UNCOVER

your

POTENTIAL

D1637116

BOOKS BY MYLES MUNROE

AVAILABLE FROM DESTINY IMAGE PUBLISHERS

UNCOVER

your

POTENTIAL

You Are MORE *than* You Realize

MYLES MUNROE

DESTINY IMAGE₀ PUBLISHERS, INC.
PO Box 310, Shippensburg, PA 17257-0310

"Promoting Inspired Lives."

Bahamas Faith Ministry
PO Box N9583
Nassau, Bahamas

For a U.S. bookstore nearest you, call 1-800-722-6774.

For more information on foreign distributors, call 717-532-3040.

Reach us on the Internet: www.destinyimage.com.

Previously published as *Understanding Your Potential*

TP ISBN: 978-0-7684-4100-0
Ebook ISBN: 978-0-7684-8866-1

For Worldwide Distribution, Printed in the U.S.A.

3 4 5 6 / 14 13 12

Contents

PREFACE

The wealthiest spot on this planet is not the oil fields of Iraq or Saudi Arabia. Neither is it the gold and diamond mines of South Africa, the uranium mines of the Soviet Union, or the silver mines of Africa. Though it may surprise you, the richest deposits on our planet lie just a few blocks from your house. They rest in your local cemetery or graveyard. Buried beneath the soil within the walls of those sacred grounds are dreams that never came to pass, songs that were never sung, books that were never written, paintings that never filled a canvas, ideas that were never shared, visions that never became reality, inventions that were never designed, plans that never went beyond the drawing board of the mind, and purposes that were never fulfilled. Our graveyards are filled with potential that remained potential. What a tragedy!

As I walk the streets of our cities, my heart frequently weeps as I encounter and observe the wasted, broken, disoriented lives of individuals who, years before, were talented, intelligent, aspiring high school classmates. During their youth they had dreams, desires, plans, and aspirations. Today they are lost in a maze of substance abuse, alcoholism, purposelessness, and poorly chosen friends. Their lives are aimless, their decisions haphazard. This enormous tragedy saddens me. What could have been has become what should have been. The wealth of dreams has been dashed into the poverty of discouragement.

Only a minute percentage of the five billion people on this planet will experience a significant portion of their true potential. Are you a candidate for contributing to the wealth of the cemetery? Ask yourself the following questions:

Who am I?

Why am I here?

How much potential do I have?

What am I capable of doing?

By what criteria should I measure my ability?

Who sets the standards?

By what process can I maximize my ability?

What are my limitations?

Within the answers to these questions lies the key to a fulfilled, effective life.

One of the greatest tragedies in life is to watch potential die untapped. Many potentially great men and women never realize their potential because they do not understand the nature and concept of the potential principle. As God has revealed to me the nature of potential, I have received a burden to teach others what I have learned.

There's a wealth of potential in you. My purpose is to help you understand that potential and get it out. You must decide if you are going to rob the world or bless it with the rich, valuable, potent, untapped resources locked away within you.

You are more than what you have done.

INTRODUCTION

The brilliant summer sun poured its liquid heat on the windswept island of the Caribbean paradise as the old village sculptor made his way to his humble home outside the village center. On his way he passed by the great white mansion of the plantation owner who, with his field workers, was felling one of the age-old trees that for generations had provided protection from the scorching sun. The old sculptor suddenly stopped and, with a twinkle in his eyes, called over the wall with a note of interest, "What will you do with those discarded stumps of wood?"

The owner replied, "These are good for nothing but firewood. I have no use for this junk."

The old sculptor begged for a piece of the "junk" wood and with care lifted the knotted tree trunk to his shoulders. With a smile of gratitude, he staggered into the distance carrying his burdensome treasure.

After entering his cottage, the old man placed the jagged piece of tree in the center of the floor. Then, in a seemingly mysterious and ceremonious manner, he walked around what the plantation owner had called "useless junk." As the old man picked up his hammer and chisel, a strange smile pierced his leathered face. Attacking the wood, he worked as though under a mandate to set something free from the gnarled, weathered trunk.

The following morning, the sun found the sculptor asleep on the floor of his cottage, clutching a beautifully sculptured bird. He had freed the bird from the bondage of the junk wood. Later he placed the bird on the railing of his front porch and forgot it.

Weeks later the plantation owner came by to visit. When he saw the bird, he asked to buy it—offering whatever price the sculptor might name. Satisfied that he had made an excellent bargain, the gentleman walked away, hugging to his breast with great pride the newly acquired treasure. The old sculptor, sitting on the steps of his simple cottage, counted his spoil and thought, *Junk is in the eyes of the beholder. Some look, but others see.*

Today there are many individuals whose lives are like the old tree. Trapped within them is a beautiful bird of potential that may never fly. Society, like the plantation owner, sees nothing in them but a useless, worthless person on his or her way to the garbage heap of life. But we must remember that one person's junk is another person's jewel.

Scientists in the field of human potential have estimated that we use as little as 10 percent of our abilities. Ninety percent of our capabilities lie dormant and wasted. It is sad that we use only a small part of our abilities and talents. Most of us have no idea how much talent and potential we possess.

Consider the life of Abraham Lincoln. His story is one of the most dramatic examples of a man struggling to release the wealth of potential locked up inside him:

He lost his job in 1832.

He was elected to the legislature in 1834.

He suffered the death of his sweetheart in 1834.

He suffered a nervous breakdown in 1836.

He was defeated for speaker of the State Legislature in 1838.

He was defeated for nomination for Congress in 1843.

He was elected to Congress in 1846.

He was rejected for the position of land officer in 1849.

He was defeated for the Senate in 1854.

He was defeated for the nomination for vice president of the United States in 1856.

He again was defeated for the Senate in 1858.

He was elected president of the United States in 1860.

Everything in life was created with potential and possesses the potential principle. In every seed there is a tree…in every bird a flock…in every fish a school…in every sheep a flock…in every cow a herd…in every boy a man…in every girl a woman…in every nation a generation. Tragedy strikes when a tree dies in a seed, a man in a boy, a woman in a girl, an idea in a mind. For untold millions, visions die unseen, songs die unsung, plans die unexecuted, and futures die buried in the past. The problems of our world go unanswered because potential remains buried.

We are responsible for the potential stored within us. We must learn to understand it and effectively use it. Too often our successes prevent us from seeking that which yet lies within us. Success becomes our enemy as we settle for what we have. Refuse to be satisfied with your last accomplishment, because potential never has a retirement plan. Do not let what you *cannot* do interfere with what you *can* do. In essence, what you see is not all there is.

Chapter 1

Everything in Life Has Potential

All people are sent to the world with limitless credit, but few draw to their full extent.

It is a tragedy to know that with over five billion people on this planet today, only a minute percentage will experience a significant fraction of their true potential. Perhaps you are a candidate for contributing to the wealth of the cemetery. Your potential was not given for you to deposit in the grave. You must understand the tremendous potential you possess and commit yourself to maximizing it in your short lifetime. What is potential, anyway?

Potential Defined

Potential is:

• Dormant ability

- Reserved power

- Untapped strength

- Unused success

- Hidden talents

- Capped capability

- All you can be but have not yet become

- All you can do but have not yet done

- How far you can reach but have not yet reached

- What you can accomplish but have not yet accomplished

Potential is unexposed ability and latent power.

Potential is therefore not what you have done, but what you are yet able to do. In other words, what you have done is no longer your potential. What you have successfully accomplished is no longer potential. It is said that unless you do something beyond what you have done, you will never grow or experience your full potential.

Potential demands that you never settle for what you have accomplished. One of the great enemies of your potential is success. In order to realize your full potential, you must never be satisfied with your last accomplishment. It is also important that you never let what you *cannot* do interfere with what you *can* do. The greatest tragedy in life is not death, but a life that never realized its full potential. You must decide today not to rob the world of the rich, valuable, potent, untapped resources locked away within you. *Potential never has a retirement plan.*

The Potential Principle

To simplify this concept, let's look at one of the most powerful elements in nature—the seed. If I held a seed in my hand and asked you, "What do I have in my hand?" what would you say? Perhaps you would answer what seems to be the obvious—a seed. However, if you understand the nature of a seed, your answer would be *fact* but not *truth.*

The truth is I hold a forest in my hand. Why? Because in every seed there is a tree, and in every tree there is fruit or flowers with seeds in them. And these seeds also have trees that have fruit that have seeds—that have trees that have fruit that have seeds, etc. In essence, *what you see is not all there is. That is potential. Not what is, but what could be.*

Don't Settle for What You Have

Nothing in life is instant. People think success is instant, but it really is not. Achieving success is a process. You are full of potential. Potential is always present, waiting to be exposed. It demands that you never settle for what you have accomplished. Oddly, one of the greatest enemies of your potential is success. Never accept success as a lifestyle—it is but a phase. Never accept an accomplishment as the end—it is but a mark in the process. There are many selves within you that lie dormant, untapped and unused. Your primary problem is that you do not think about yourself as having even greater potential.

You *can* maximize the potential within you. You are not yet what you are supposed to be—though you may be pleased with what you now are. Don't accept your present state in life as final, because it is just that, a state. Don't be satisfied with your last accomplishment, because there are many accomplishments yet to be perfected. Since you are full of potential, you should not be the same person next year that you are this year.

◆ ◆ ◆

There are many selves within you that lie dormant, untapped and unused.

◆ ◆ ◆

You should always be looking for what is not yet visible. There is more inside you than is evident on the outside. On the other hand, humankind is often satisfied with what we have—at least if not satisfied, we think there is nothing better. Thus we settle for what we have. Do you?

Therein lies the tragedy of life. The minute we begin to settle down and be satisfied with what we have, we lose the possibility of revealing what is really inside us. Too often we die without exploring the gifts, abilities, and successes that lay hidden within us. Our thoughts, ideas, and possibilities are not used. We fail to realize the vast potential that is stored within us. We are like batteries in a radio that is never played—our potential is wasted.

Suppose...

Suppose Shakespeare had died before he wrote his poems and plays—the potential of Macbeth would have been buried. Suppose Michelangelo had died before he painted the Sistine Chapel or DaVinci the Mona Lisa—the beauty of their paintings would have been lost. Suppose Mozart had died with all that music inside. Or suppose a world without women like Joan of Arc, Emily Dickinson, Amelia Earhart, Helen Keller, Florence Nightingale, Queen Isabella, or Mother Teresa.

Can you imagine how many great works of art, music, and literature are buried in the graveyard near your house? Can you imagine how many solutions to the problems we face today are buried with someone you knew? People die without getting out their full potential. They fail to use all that was stored in them for the benefit of the world.

Don't Die With My Things!

I wonder what would have happened if your father had died before you were conceived or your mother before you were born.

What would the world have lost if you had not been born? What will the world lack because you fail to live out your potential? Will you carry songs, books, inventions, cures, or discoveries to your grave?

————— ◆ ◆ ◆ —————

**What would the world have lost
if you had not been born?**

————— ◆ ◆ ◆ —————

Our teens are committing suicide. I wonder who they were supposed to be and what they were supposed to do that we will never know. Have we lost some great leaders? Was your grandchild's professor or another Martin Luther King Jr. among them?

Everything in life has the potential to fulfill its purpose. People who die without achieving their full potential rob their generation of their latent ability. Many have robbed me— they've also robbed you. To die with ability is irresponsible.

Perhaps you are wasting your life doing nothing with all you have. There are skills, talents, and unique aspects of personality packaged in you for the good of the world— use them. We will never know the wealth planted in you until you bring it up. There's always something in you that we haven't yet seen. Release your ability before you die. Use the power and strength within you for the good of yourself and others. I believe there are books, songs, art works, businesses, poems, inventions, cures, and investments in you that are intended for my children and future grandchildren to benefit from and enjoy.

New From Old

Consider this: Innovation does not create new raw materials. All of the raw materials are already created. Innovation recombines them in fresh ways. Everything that we call "new" is a new grouping of old things. The exact combination and the timing of the combination may be new, but the raw materials are not new.

Everything necessary to invest in the next new thing is already present in the world. Innovation enables someone to see old things with new eyes and to combine them in new ways for new purposes.

When you go to the store and buy a new pair of shoes, it is an old cowhide that has been cut and stretched and stitched and soled. When you buy a book, the cover and the pages have been made from a plant. When you buy a new suit, it is old sheep wool, "reformatted." When you buy a beautiful new wooden dining room table, it is not as new as you might think because it is really an old tree, worked over and changed into a table. When you buy a "new" car, it is a combination of old metals, petroleum products, and so forth. Things and people can be re-purposed. But do you know what your purpose really is?

Who Are You?

Who am I? Why am I here? Where did I come from? What was I born to do? What can I do? Where do I fit? Why am I different? What is my potential? Where am I going? Why did I come to this planet?—are universal questions that haunt every human being. Each of us must find the answers to these questions of purpose if we are going to enjoy a meaningful, effective, fulfilling life.

Purpose and fulfilling our potential are keys to life. Without purpose, life has no meaning. There are millions today busy making a living, but they experience very little of life. If your goal in life is to be wealthy so you can retire, you have embarked on a depressing journey to nowhere. If your vision for life is measured by status, your upkeep will be your downfall. Vision is buried in purpose. Without knowledge of purpose, life becomes an endless string of activities with little or no significance. Like a rider on a rocking horse, life without purpose makes much motion but no progress.

A World Without Purpose

A lack of purpose and the impending tragedy that results from its absence is found not only in people but in all things. When elements of nature lose their purpose, chaos and destruction are the results. When nations, societies, communities, organizations, friendships, marriages, clubs, churches, countries, or tribes lose their sense of purpose and significance, then confusion, frustration, discouragement, disillusionment, and corporate suicide—whether gradual or instant—reign. *Purpose is the master of motivation and the mother of commitment.* It is the source of enthusiasm and the womb of perseverance.

Purpose gives birth to hope and instills the passion to act. It is the common denominator that gives every creature an element of distinction. This guiding sense of purpose is more than an orientation toward a goal. Rather, it is a deep awareness that a common vision encompasses all life and existence. Without this vision, we can only exist. We feel no passion for living—neither do we have a reason to wake up in the morning.

———◆—◆———

Purpose gives birth to hope and instills the passion to act on fulfilling your potential.

———◆—◆———

Thousands of years ago, a king known as the wisest man who ever lived stated, "Meaningless! Meaningless! …Utterly meaningless! Everything is meaningless." This was his conclusion after years of observing life, activities, plans, and achievements apart from a sense of personal and corporate purpose. These words and their sad echo have returned to haunt us nearly six thousand years later. We face a world that acts like a spaceship that has lost its flight plan.

Planet Earth is like a mother whose children have lost all sense of direction and all value in life. Globally speaking, everything is in motion. Mergers and acquisitions, deregulations and changing agencies of control, information technologies, and international competition all alter the shape and thrust of our economies and the way we do business. Changing demographics, realigned industry structures, new strategic alliances, innovative technologies, unaccustomed modes of working, and the volatility of stock markets demand a fresh approach to commerce. Increasing competition, the shrinking of the world into one large global village, the move toward freer markets in former communist countries, and the reality of the European Common Market alter the way we deal with the world and it deals with us. Many industrialized nations are being transformed into Third World states as numerous people migrate from undeveloped nations.

Long-established ideologies are evaporating in the fires of revolutionary changes. Institutions long held sacred are crumbling under the weight of social pressure. In almost every nation, the situation is the same. There is political confusion, ideological frustration, social unrest, economic uncertainty, moral bankruptcy, institutionalized corruption, and disillusionment with religion. All inhabit an environment of fragile diplomacy.

The world has become an incubator of stress, depression, hopelessness, and fear. It seems that the kingdoms and the governments of this world are bankrupt. They no longer offer innovative solutions for these ever-increasing problems. Industrialized nations are as fragile as Third World nations. The tremendous changes in national and international situations, and the economic, political, social, and cultural transitions that have accompanied these changes, now present a totally different global equation.

There is also a generation in every nation that seems to have lost its sense of purpose. They are out of touch with the values, morals, and convictions that build strong families, secure communities, healthy societies, and prosperous nations. Thus, the moral fabric of most societies is being stretched and tested to its outer limits. In every nation, the concern is the same. Many of the time-weathered institutions of the industrial states are being tried by challenges that threaten to transform tradition and demand creative and innovative responses.

Hope Through Potential's Purpose

There is the great hope, though, for the world as we recognize the potential and purpose in all people and things to be fulfilled by combining and putting some of the already-created things together in a new way. Don't limit your potential by thinking that there is nothing new under the sun. Don't give up until you have lived out the full extent of your potential, because you have no right to die with my things. Don't rob the next generations of the wealth, treasures, and tremendous gifts buried deep within you.

- If you want to succeed, strike out on new paths. Don't travel the worn paths of accepted success.

- No one can climb beyond the limitations of his or her own belief. Every day sends to the grave obscure men and women whom fear prevented from realizing their true and full potential.

- Failure is not the absence of success. Failure is the neglect of trying.

- What you see is not all there is. There is potential in everything.

What you have done is no longer your potential. Potential is what you can do but have not yet done.

Consider, for a moment, a rose. In the spring before the rose bush blooms, it is ugly. Thorns cover the stems and tiny, hard green things stick out among the leaves. After a few weeks, these little green things slowly begin to open until you can see the color of the petals. Then the bud begins to open and the individual petals become visible. Still, the rose is not what it yet can be. It has not reached the height of its beauty. There comes a point when the fully opened rose reaches perfection. It can be no more beautiful.

Its shape and color are in perfect harmony. After perfection is reached, death and decay set in. The flowers whither and brown until the petals fall from the bush. It fulfills its purpose and then naturally dies.

Nothing—and no one—should die until its purpose is fulfilled.

Principles

1. You were created with potential.

2. Nothing in life is instant.

3. Everything in life has the potential to fulfill its purpose.

4. Don't be satisfied with what you now are.

5. Don't die without using your full potential.

6. The greatest threat to progress is your last successful accomplishment.

Chapter 2

THE VISIBLE AND INVISIBLE

Transforming ideas into action.

Everything in life was created with potential and possesses the potential principle. Creation abounds with potential. All we now see was once in an invisible state. Everything that we have ever seen first existed in an invisible state. (Please note that invisible does not mean nonexistent.)

All the buildings we see and the businesses we frequent—people making money and investing money—all that stuff began as ideas. We couldn't see them because they were in somebody's mind. The stores where we shop, also everything on the shelves and racks in those stores, began as ideas in someone's mind. They didn't exist before, yet they did. Although they weren't present in their current form, they existed as lumber and concrete and nails, cotton and wool, flax, steel, and pulleys and motors.

Someone had an idea. Through work they put their idea into things that are visible. Today they accept your money in exchange for the reality of their ideas. Everything starts in the invisible state. Everything we now see used to be unseen.

There's a guy in China right now who is thinking about the idea you thought was yours. I believe that when the idea came from God, many people got it. Many received the idea from the same Source. Until that idea is transformed by action, I believe that ideas will be leaked into men and women worldwide.

We are pregnant with much. We are full of imagination, having the potential power to be more than we visibly are. There are dreams, visions, plans, and ideas in us that need to be released.

Many Look, Few See

A sculptor works in a very interesting way. I'm an artist of sorts, so I have a bit of an understanding about how artists work. One thing I have learned is that you never argue with an artist until he or she is finished. Don't discuss anything with a painter or a sculptor until the work is completed. An artist can be very rude if disturbed before the work is accomplished—an artist sees differently from those who are not artists.

An artist can walk by the stone in your front yard and see a figure in it. An artist may stop by your house and beg you for a stone you have walked past many times without noticing. In fact, dogs may have been doing stuff on it. You may even have planned to get rid of it because it's a nuisance. But the artist walks into your yard and sees something beautiful in that stone beyond what you can imagine.

Two months later when the artist invites you to his workshop he says, "Do you see that? Do you know where that came from?"

"England…France?" you ask.

"No," says the artist. "It came from your yard."

"Do you mean…?"

"Yes."

"Five hundred dollars, please."

You were sitting on $500. The dogs were doing stuff on $500. No one could see the potential in the rock.

Another Story

I was in an Asian antique store one day that had beautiful furniture and trinkets. As I walked through the store, I picked up four or five bowls of different sizes and shapes. I thought, "These are nice dishes to eat from." So I took them to the attendant and said, "How much are these bowls?"

The attendant, who was Korean, replied adamantly, "These aren't bowls."

"Oh, I'm sorry," I said. "What are they?"

"These are ceremonial dishes for a Korean wedding," he replied.

"Excuse me," I said and replaced the dishes. Then I picked up some sort of thing that flapped and made noise that sounded like music to me and said, "This is a good musical instrument. How much is it?"

Again the attendant replied, "That's not a musical instrument. This is used for incense when you go to the temple."

Again I said, "Excuse me," and continued my search. After I had missed four or five times, I asked him to go with me as I walked through the shop. As we looked at the many interesting items on display, I constantly asked him, "What's this? What's that? How is this used?" The attendant, who had grown up in Korea, knew the purpose for everything that I asked about. What looked like a stool, for example, was really a chest of drawers. Indeed, it would have broken had I sat on it.

Because he was part of the culture, the clerk knew the purpose for everything in the whole store. He did not need to guess at the purpose of each item like I had done, (I was wrong 80 percent of the time), because he knew from experience how each piece was used.

Had I simply bought the objects I liked without asking what they were and how they were to be used, I would have ruined some beautiful pieces. Since I didn't know their purpose, abuse was inevitable no matter how sincere I was. My friends and family would have misused them as well because they wouldn't have been any more knowledgeable concerning the purpose of the item than I was. Just because we all would have used them the same way wouldn't have made our use right. In ignorance, we all would have abused them.

You Are Not Junk

There are many people who are being passed by because others don't see what is in them. My job is to stop you and say: "Can you see what's in you? Do you know your potential? Do you know that you are not just someone born in a ghetto over the hill? There's a wealth of potential in you."

A sculptor sees so differently. They say Michelangelo used to walk around a block of marble for days—just walking around it, talking to himself. First he would see things in the rock; then he would use his inherent skills and talents and produce a masterpiece.

When the world dumps and rejects you, and you land on the garbage heap of the world, stand resolved to be hopeful and courageous. You are a person of great worth. Don't ever let anybody throw you away. You are not junk. Don't accept the opinions of others because they do not see what great and valuable potential is inside you.

Insight Into Potential

A long time ago, there was a group of people who wanted a king to rule over them. A representative was sent to the home of a man who had many sons—ones the father was sure would make the perfect king. Before the rep came, the father dressed up all his sons—the handsome one, the tall one, the curly-haired one, the strong one, the well-spoken one.

All the sons twirled out before the representative, from the greatest to the least. He presented his sons: "This is my intelligent son who graduated from the University of I Don't Know What." After the guy gave a speech, the rep said, "No." The next son came out dressed like he stepped out of *GQ* magazine and the rep said, "No." A third son gave a nice speech about philosophy and again the rep said, "No." Finally, after the father had paraded all of his sons before him, he said, "I'm sorry. None of these is the right choice for king. Do you have any other sons?"

"Well, yes. I do have a little boy, my youngest son. He's just a little runt who's out taking care of the sheep. He's not dressed up like my other sons, nor have his hands been manicured and his body scented with perfumes from the

East. This guy's really smelly because he's been with the sheep for quite some time."

"Bring him. Let me look at him."

So the father sent for his youngest son. As soon as the young son walked into the house, a little boy, the representative said, "I have found the guy I'm looking for."

The rep chose the son who was out working. He was busy—busy people are chosen people. Most of us look, but we don't see. Were you the black sheep in your family? Has your family told you that you are a nobody? Have you been put off and put out and told so many times that you will amount to nothing that you have begun to believe it? Do you feel like the black sheep?

You are probably the one with the most potential. There are deep things, positive things within you that others can't see. They look at you and see a nobody; but you are a worthwhile somebody.

You may spend your whole life competing with others—trying to prove that you are somebody—and still feel like nobody. Be free from that today! You do not have to live with that wrong mindset any longer. You don't have to try to be somebody, because you are somebody.

Intentions and Uniqueness

Many of the inventions humankind has produced would be misunderstood if only the invention were considered and not the intention of the inventor. In other words, the person who created the refrigerator had in his mind what it was supposed to be used for. He did not intend that it should be used for a trap in the backyard for a kid to be locked in and die from suffocation. Even though thousands of children have died in refrigerators, that was not the inventor's intention.

The automobile is tearing out lampposts all over the world and destroying people's homes and lives. But Henry Ford, who first developed the assembly line to mass produce the automobile, never thought about it that way. He was thinking about transporting people and helping the human race to become a mobile community. He started us thinking about trolleys and trains and buses. The many people who have died through accidents and derailments were not part of his intention. They were not in Mr. Ford's mind when he designed His famous Model T automobile.

You will never discover who you were meant to be if you use another person to find yourself. You will never know what you can do by using what I've done to measure your ability. You will never know why you exist if you use my existence to measure it. All you will see is what I've done or who I am. If you want to know who you are, the key to understanding life is in the Source of life, not in the life itself.

We are always full of potential. Our potential is the dormant ability, reserved power, untapped strength, and unused success designed into each of us. What I see when I look at you is not all you are. It is only what you have become so far. Your potential is much greater than what you are right now. What you will become is much more than we could ever believe now.

How you feel or what others say about you is not important. You are who you are; and you are more than you can possibly imagine. You are the only one who can limit your potential.

Coward or Warrior?

Another story is about a frightened young man named Gideon. Gideon obviously thought the angel who called him a mighty warrior was talking to someone else. The angel who appeared to him said, "Oh mighty man of war power!" That means, "Oh great warrior!" The angel didn't say, "Oh, coward. Do you know you have strength?" Nor did the angel say, "Oh black man, do you know that you can be like the white man?" The angel just came in and announced what he saw: "Oh mighty man of war power."

Think about it. Warrior? At that point, Gideon was hiding from the enemy, trying to separate some wheat from the chaff so he wouldn't starve. He was doing it underground so no one could see him. When the angel said, "You are a brave man," Gideon started looking around to see who the angel was talking to.

Gideon thought he was a coward. But the One who sent the angel knew Gideon to be a great warrior and pronounced what He saw.

Stop Believing What Others Say

Too often we believe the lies we are told. We believe that we are "no good" and worthless.

Remember that the seed of every tree is in the fruit of the tree. That means the blessings of the Third World nations are in the Third World nations, and the prosperity of the United States is in the United States. When we become concerned about our individual lives or the corporate life of our countries, we come up with all kinds of schemes and plans to solve the problem. But the answer is not in a multitude of systems and programs. The answer is right inside of us. It's our attitudes that make the difference.

No one can make you rowdy or careless or thoughtless. You are rowdy and careless and thoughtless because you choose to be. So stop it! Stop being rowdy, stop being careless, stop being thoughtless. Only you can control how you act. You've got the potential to be considerate and sensitive.

If we become so busy agreeing with what others call us, we miss seeing our true potential. When we start believing what others call us, we are in big trouble. Then we throw our hands up in despair and refuse to try. People call us lazy, so we become lazy. People call us careless or stupid or clumsy, so we become careless or stupid or clumsy. Watch it! What others look at is not important. Who we are depends on what we see within ourselves.

Do you believe you could walk into a prison and meet some of the greatest men and women in the world? Can you think that way? They made mistakes. They made misjudgments. They made poor decisions. But that doesn't invalidate their potential. It doesn't destroy who they can be. In that jail there may be a murderer on death row. But there are also authors, leaders, and great world changers.

Only you know your true potential. Have you failed? Pick yourself back up and start again. Success is in your hands, your attitude, and in your mindset. If you believe what other people are saying—maybe that you are no good—you'll never be somebody.

Rather, see yourself as a valuable jewel—a diamond in the rough. Just keep on believing that. Keep on moving forward toward your goal. Remember that there is something in you more precious than what others have said about you. The sculptor never gives up until he or she gets out of the rock what the sculptor sees.

There is something in you more precious than what others have said about you.

I have a piece of wooden sculpture in my home that I did about fifteen years ago. The sculpture isn't what I intended it to be because as I was chiseling out the image that I had seen in the tree, part of it was knocked off by too much pressure. Because that part dropped off, I could no longer create the image that I had intended. So I looked at the piece of wood again. I walked around it thinking, "I've gotta change my concept a little." I had to rethink how to retain the beauty of the sculpture though I had lost an important part of the wood.

Something Beautiful

Eventually, I modified my design. But I am the only person who knows that piece of sculpture was made from a modified design. The modification is not evident in the finished form. If I showed you the piece, you wouldn't even notice what I'm talking about. People have admired that piece of wood for many years. They look at it and say, "Wow! This is beautiful." And I never tell them that what they see is not what they were originally supposed to see.

That piece of sculpture sitting in my home reminds me of your life and mine. Parts of our lives have been knocked off by our past. We've done some dumb things that have messed up the beauty intended. But instead of discarding ourselves and our potential because we have not turned out as first intended—including our marred, chipped, rusted, and knocked-off past—we can be transformed into something beautiful. When people see us now, they won't believe what we used to be!

When people look at you and think you are the best thing that ever came down the pike, don't tell them what you used to be. Just say, "Thank you very much."

In every piece of stone a sculptor sees a figure. But we never see it until he or she takes it out. Whereas we may see only an old stump of a tree on the side of the road, a wood sculptor sees a beautiful piece that we would pay thousands of dollars to own. What looks like garbage to the nonartistic person is a treasure to the artist.

Your IQ doesn't measure who you are. Your designer clothes don't measure who you are. The size of your home or bank account don't measure who you are. Your friends and family's comments don't measure who you are. Thinking positively and knowing you are full of positive potential is who you are and can be—the best is yet to come!

What if...

If I went to a contractor and asked him to construct a building for me, his first question would be, "What is your purpose for this building?" That would be the underlying concern for the whole project: *Why do I want this building to exist and what do I want it to accomplish? What is its potential?* Thus, establishing the purpose for the building is the first priority.

After that is settled, the contractor would probably say to me: "Let me see your plans. I need to see how your architect designed the building." As he looked over the plans, the contractor would consider whether the plans revealed a design that would allow the building to function in a manner that would meet the determined purpose.

Let's say, for example, that I wanted the contractor to erect a building that could be used for providing medical care. The building must, therefore, meet the needs of doctors, nurses, X-ray and lab technicians, patients, and so on, and the design must facilitate that performance. Thus, the purpose for the building determines its function, and the function necessitates design. If the building is to function as an accountant's office, its design will be quite different from that of a hospital.

Let's consider another example. If my wife has fabric (potential) and wants to sew a dress (purpose), she will design the dress to meet her needs for either summer or winter wear (function). She might make a dress for winter out of heavy fabric and style it with a snug fit, a high neck, long sleeves, and fur trim. A summer dress, on the other hand, might be cut from a lightweight material and fashioned with a loose fit, a low neckline, short sleeves, and lace or net trim. The winter dress, that functions to keep her warm, would reveal that in its design. Likewise, the summer dress would be styled to keep her cool and comfortable during hot weather.

In essence, *what* you are and *how* you are was predetermined by *why* you are. Your design is perfect for your purpose and fulfilling your potential.

Principles

1. All things have the same components and essence as their source.

2. Everything with life was created with potential.

3. You will never know yourself by listening to what others say about you.

4. Your potential is much greater than what you are right now.

5. You are the only one who can limit your potential.

6. Know that the best you can be is awaiting you.

Chapter 3

SEEKING SELF AND WISDOM

*When people limit what they **can** be,*
*they limit what they **will** be.*

Deep within each person is a yearning to become more—more successful, more content, more intelligent, more healthy, more loving, more handsome or pretty—always more. But over the years of various attempts and failures at improving our lives, we finally convince ourselves that we are worthless, rotten, incapable people. We become satisfied with life as is, and abandon having more.

Although there may be family, friends, or even spouses who say things or do things that hold us back from becoming "more," the only one who really has that power is the person who looks back at you in the mirror. No one else can steal our potential—only we can keep it hidden, sometimes for a lifetime.

You Are Not Ugly!

The deceiver within us distorts our self-concept. We don't like ourselves for a variety of unfounded reasons, and we become professional "cover-ups." We don't like our physical bodies. Yuk! I don't like how skinny I am, how fat I am, how my hair grows, how my eyes are shaped, how my lips are. I don't like my black, brown, red, yellow, or white skin. So we try to cover up what we don't like. It is strange how we work on things. If our hair is curly, we straighten it. If our skin is too pale, we tan it. We don't like what we see in the mirror. Nobody is satisfied with themselves. We all walk around thinking, *Why can't I be more like him? Why can't I look more like her?*

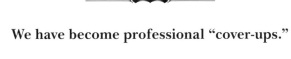

We have become professional "cover-ups."

This self-depreciating attitude is unhealthy. Our potential has been distorted so that we don't want to be black or tall or fat. We don't want to have curly hair or fat lips or small eyes. We have accepted this ploy to destroy our esteem for the beautiful people we really are.

Because we do not like ourselves, we do all kinds of dumb things to ourselves, including limiting our opportunities. If you love yourself, you are not going to lower your standards. You will not sell yourself to anybody or sell yourself short. You won't allow anybody to buy you—you are too expensive.

You Are Not Dumb!

A self-depreciating attitude also destroys our confidence in our true intelligence. Wisdom and intelligence can be two completely different things. Someone may be full of common sense wisdom but may have never completed college. Someone else may have a Ph.D. but is unable to balance their checkbook. Intelligence and wisdom are doled out according to how a person comprehends the importance of both. This is not learned. It is discerned. This knowledge isn't found in any book; it's a deeper knowledge. Your real intelligence is not studied; it is discerned. Wow!

◆ ◆ ◆

**Your real intelligence is not studied;
it is discerned.**

◆ ◆ ◆

Many have become victims of education. We look to books and movies and the words of others—what we can see, hear, taste, feel, and touch—to gain knowledge. Those things became our sources of information. When we forget to discern our own real intelligence, we look outside ourselves to find knowledge.

You Will Become!

Always looking to others for approval or acceptance sometimes limits our life potential. Many times they, knowingly or unknowingly, destroy any possibility that we might have to become more than we already are: Teachers in our classrooms call us stupid. Brothers and sisters call us dumb and "no good." Parents tell us, "You'll never be anything."

Sometimes we set ourselves up. We chop up our self-confidence and slam the door on our potential by convincing ourselves that we really are nothing: "I'll never rise above my family's status. I'll never go beyond my neighborhood. I'll never be any more than my mom or dad. I don't stand a chance." When we think and speak these types of negative thoughts, they keep us down; it's deceptive thinking.

Seek an Abundant Life

We must free ourselves of those things that retard, distort, and short-circuit everything we are capable of being and doing.

We think life is what we have now. No! In the Greek, the same word is used for abundance as is used for fountain. You need to take the cap off your well—to unclog the true you—to open up the capacity of who you are and who you can be. You are going to have an unprecedented oil spill. This thing is going to explode. The potential within you is welling up and when it blows, it will never stop spilling out!

You are finally going to meet your real self. All you have done for the past ten years that made you think you were somebody is but a trickle. You haven't changed the world, friend. You haven't done anything yet! But there is a fountain, an abundance of life, welling up in you so you can do and be something. It begins when you realize that you are an amazing person, created to do amazing things.

Uncapping the Well

No one in the world stifles and clogs up and caps your potential like you do. Unknowingly, you think up schemes to make yourself believe that you can be nothing more than you have already been. You have the power to destroy this scheme, to unclog the well and become your true self.

Daily you must convince yourself about who you really are. For example, you are meant to use all the gifts and talents and skills that are uniquely yours. You were not meant to live in poverty and hunger or sickness. You were meant to live an abundant life. Speak that into your mirror each morning. Believe it.

The Cap and the Crowbar

When others tell you that you aren't going to amount to anything: You aren't going to be anything. You can't do anything. You will always be what you now are. You must pull from deep within to undo those negative claims. You can be anything you think. You have the power to rip the top right off your capped well. Go ahead, gush forth!

Thus, a tremendous struggle goes on within us—one destroyer uses a cap to hold in our potential, the other uses a crowbar to yank off the top and allow the wealth within to pour out. Every time the one with the crowbar yanks off the top, the other runs around with the cap in hand. The minute we give him a chance, he covers up the well again. The struggle is continual. Each day we experience the tension.

What's Clogging Your Well?

Are there things in your life that have been holding you back from the things you should be doing? Are you a potential leader in your community but you're full of alcohol and you're lying in the gutter? Has cocaine stolen your potential to be the top student in your class? Is your brain all messed up so you can't even think any more? Are you in danger of being kicked out of school though you were an A student before you took the stuff? Have you run off with a dumb guy and gotten pregnant? Do you have to drop out of school and give up your visions of becoming a doctor, lawyer, scientist, teacher, or an agricultural expert? Have you clogged up your potential because of unwise choices?

Did you have a business that was going well, with limitless potential, until somebody said to you, "I want you to sell drugs for me. You'll make a lot more money than you do in this lame business"? So you became greedy. You went ahead and sold the drugs—only you were caught and now you have a criminal record and your business is destroyed.

**Unclog your well and
release your potential.**

Greed and pride clogs our potential. This duo messes up the plan for us to reach our destiny. It takes away the "And they lived happily ever after" and replaces it with "And they struggled but didn't make it through the day." Don't let that be the last chapter in your book—know that you are flowing within with potential. The problem is that you don't know your potential. You have been destroyed by greed and pride, which is stunting your growth.

You can destroy the works that are holding you down.

The Wrong Place

One afternoon a mother took her son to the local elementary school for soccer practice. She returned an hour and a half later to find an angry, tearful child. When she asked him what was wrong, he said, "My practice wasn't here today. It was at the park. We must have read the schedule wrong. So, I had to sit and watch the other teams practice. It was so boring! Now I'm afraid my coach won't let me play in the game on Saturday because I missed practice."

Most of us have had the experience of being at the wrong place. We've waited at one entrance to the store while our friends were looking for us at another. Or we've waited at a customer service desk to exchange a purchase, only to find that we had to go to the department where the purchase was made. Such experiences are disturbing because we cannot achieve what we set out to do.

Such frustration is minor compared to the turmoil created by our competition to excel and reach a position of prestige and honor. This desire to get ahead is a compelling passion in our world. Every person has been bitten by this aspiration to rise in status. We are preoccupied with the status quo, and we seek to gain status symbols. We want the best for ourselves with little or no concern for those we climb over in our pursuit for a position of power. The desire for status is an age-old problem. From the time we are very young, we learn to do the things that enhance our status and bring us prominence and prestige.

Status literally means "the state of us." Webster[1] defines it as a "condition or position with regard to the law." Thus, status is position. Webster also describes status as "the position of an individual in relation to another"—showing that status has to do with rank—and "the state or condition of affairs." Status is not just a random ordering of things, but a careful positioning that reveals the relationships between people or the parts of a whole.

When I went to junior high school, I wanted to become an A student because A students are respected and appreciated. Everybody speaks to you, and the teachers love you. In other words, my purpose for trying to attain the A student status had nothing to do with a desire to help others. I was out to grab all I could for myself.

Similar things happen in the workplace. Perhaps you are part of an office where fake games are played. Somebody's always making the coffee, vacuuming the floor, or making copies. Now all of these are necessary tasks, but the motive behind the action is of primary importance. Are these things being done as a service to others, or are they a way to gain special recognition and advancement?

Humility and consideration for others occurs most easily when you value your position as well as the positions of others. A visible position does not equal greater value. Each is to do his or her task to the best of his or her ability to benefit the whole. Those with leadership potential or who are in leadership receive that status to strengthen everyone.

Wisdom Protects

Wisdom protects us from the dangers of knowledge. Potential is dormant ability. (The word *dormant* means what is just lying there below its full strength, unused.) It is also reserved power, untapped strength, and unused success. Potential is everything that a thing is, that has not yet been seen or manifested.

Everything in life begins as potential. All things have the potential to fulfill themselves. There is no fulfillment in life without understanding the reason for being. If we want to know the real potential of something, we first have to know what that thing was created to do.

So if you have a seed in your hand, a kernel of corn, or a pea, you will never get the seeds complete fulfillment until you know that there is a plant inside that seed. It is only as we look beyond the seed to the plant that we understand its true potential.

Too often, however, we look only at what we presently have. We look at our last dollar and say, "All I have is one dollar." No. That is not all you have. If you only knew the potential of that dollar. If you take that dollar and put it into a certain condition, it will multiply.

**The potential of everything is related
to its purpose for being.**

Before we can understand the potential of a thing or person, we first must know the conditions under which it was meant to exist. Thus the most important thing for you and me, as human beings, is to try and find out for the rest of our lives what the purpose is for everything in life. That is our main goal. Unless we ask ourselves, "What is the purpose for everything in life?" we will die without having experienced the potential of everything. We will miss the ultimate wisdom.

When somebody tells you they are wise, don't get carried away. Although they may have wisdom, it might not be the right kind of wisdom.

The World's Wisdom

Some wisdom is corrupt. Any wisdom that does not fulfill its original purpose is foolishness. So if you are wise and you can really figure things out, but you use it to steal, you are foolish. If you are a very skillful musician, but you use your gift to create lewdness and sensuality, and to cause people to go into perversion, that is foolishness. If you know that the power, talents, and gifts you have are yours to use for good or evil, your wisdom becomes foolishness if you chose to destroy rather than build up.

---◆ ◆ ◆---

**Any wisdom that does not fulfill
its original purpose is foolishness.**

---◆ ◆ ◆---

49

Although much of the wisdom of the world is foolishness, it is still wisdom. It's a perverted wisdom used by perverters to blind us to its very foolishness. The Internet, 3D movies, smart phones, and all the other amazing technology available these days took much intelligence to invent, but how many lives have been destroyed because of the criminal and perverted ways some have chosen to use them.

Your Secret Wisdom

You have a secret wisdom that was placed in you before you were born—a potential something—a wisdom to know who you are and what you were created to be and do. That potential something is a hidden understanding that follows neither the wisdom of our society nor the insights of our leaders. Unlike the wisdom of the world, which is worthless, this secret wisdom is the key to understanding your potential.

Many people die without unveiling their wealth of wisdom. They die in total foolishness, without experiencing the life that dwells within. What a pity! They have missed discovering their secret wisdom. *Secret* here does not mean to be withheld from. It rather has the meaning of to have never known existed. There is a difference. This secret wisdom is something we never knew existed within us.

━━━━◆◆◆━━━━

You were born rich with wisdom.

━━━━◆◆◆━━━━

I know you may find that hard to accept—perhaps you think I am a mad man. But the truth is you'll be shocked when you understand who you really are. You don't know what you have inside that you are selling so cheaply. You have a secret wisdom, a wisdom that you should be using to discover your potential.

None of the rulers of this world understand it, nor have they ever understood it. If only we could understand who we are. We keep thinking that the life we left behind is better than the life toward which we are headed. We are constantly dipping into the ways and wisdom of the world to try and solve our present situations. But the world does not know the wisdom and potential destined for us. They don't understand it and sometimes they resent that we have a secret wisdom that carries us forward toward our unique destiny.

Your eyes can't see, your ears can't hear, neither can your mind imagine the future that awaits you. It's totally beyond what you can understand. If you could see through your eyes what you were created to be, you'd change your life. If you could hear through your ears or perceive through your mind what you were created to be you would, but unfortunately you can't. Your situation sounds hopeless: No eyes have seen it; no ears have heard it; no mind has conceived it. Your eyes and ears and mind cannot help you understand what was prepared for you before you were born. If they could, you'd shape up!

The Deep Things

Most people have not seen their secret wisdom, nor have they heard about it. They have never even thought about the stuff because there are certain things we cannot understand. They are so deep within our potential that we need help to drag them out.

Deep within our wells, a clog has formed and blocks the entryway. There is wealth within the well—there inside your being. There is wealth in your personality; wealth in your smile; wealth in your mind and spirit. But it has been clogged up and capped off by greed, pride, selfishness, and lack of self-esteem.

When you were born, the cap over your potential was firmly in place. You may never know what is buried beneath that cap. I believe that billions of dollars of wealth are buried within you, but you are not aware of it. You're walking along cool, but you don't know who you are. You don't understand that what you see is merely the shadow of your potential.

Your capped potential is like a new battery. You came into the world full of the ability to run the whole thing. But you're just sitting there. Your stored power isn't being used. Like a battery that needs acidic water inside it before it can really fulfill its purpose, you need something to unleash the potential locked inside you. You have the key that allows all the dormant power within you to come to life.

You have the key that allows all the dormant power within you to come to life.

Forget what others have told you about who you can be. That's a joke. Don't even consider what they have said. That is not all you can be, because the deepest things you can know about yourself are not in your mind or your emotions or even in your body. They are in your spirit. The deepest things you can know about yourself are what you get from your spirit.

Only you can capture the wealth of your potential. Until you take a deep look within yourself and stop the negative talk coming at you and coming from within you, you will only walk around confused, thinking, *There's gotta be more. There's gotta be more.* When you hunger for the deep things, you will not be satisfied until you realize the secret wisdom. You will never be satisfied, because there is something inside you that continually calls out for more.

Do you want to know how cute you can be? Do you want to know how smart you are? Your potential is buried. We may think having regular people go to the moon is great—but wait until you see what even greater things are going to be announced. There is so much potential within all people!

Uncapping the well unravels the knots that have bound your thoughts, removes the streaks that have blurred your vision, and clears the debris that has hidden your potential. Working like a sculptor, you can bring out the beauty hidden deep within your being, because that is the real you.

It is my dream that you will see with your eyes and hear with your ears things you have never seen or heard before. Conceive with your mind thoughts that never before have occurred to you. Live the rest of your life building an atmosphere of hope and confidence that permeates deep into the wells of your potential and pulls it to the top of your senses. Drink deeply, growing in the knowledge of who you really are.

Principles

1. Greed and pride clogs your potential.

2. You can experience abundant, refreshing, new life.

3. The potential of everything is related to its purpose for being.

4. The wisdom of the world is a foolish, corrupt wisdom.

5. Uncapping the well unravels the knots that have bound your thoughts, removes the streaks that have blurred your vision, and clears the debris that has hidden your potential.

Endnote

1. *Merriam-Webster's Collegiate Dictionary Eleventh Edition* (Springfield, MA: Merriam-Webster, Incorporated, 2008).

Chapter 4

WHY WERE YOU BORN?

No one can make you feel inferior without your consent.
—Eleanor Roosevelt

The deepest craving of the human spirit is to find a sense of significance and relevance. The search for relevance in life is the ultimate pursuit of humanity. Conscious or unconscious, admitted or not, this internal passion is what motivates and drives every human being, either directly or indirectly. It directs decisions, controls behavior, and dictates responses to the environment.

This need for significance is the cause of great tragedies. Many suicides and attempted suicides owe their manifestation to this compelling need. Many mass murderers and serial killers confess the relationship of their antisocial behavior to their need to feel important or to experience a sense of self-worth.

This passion for relevance and a sense of signifi-cance makes one race or ethnic group elevate itself above another. It also gives birth to prejudice and causes the fabrication of erroneous perceptions that result in grave injustices and the conception of abominable dreams and inhuman behavior. It also gives birth to tyrants and dicta-tors who easily sacrifice the sacredness of human life and dignity for a temporary sense of significance.

This desperate desire to feel important and relevant to one's existence also causes the sacrifice of common sense, good judgment, moral standards, and basic human values. Many individuals have sacrificed excellent reputa-tions and years of character-building lifestyles for the sake of advancement to a desired position or a place of recogni-tion and fame in their society or workplace so they could feel important and worthwhile.

This passion for a sense of significance and meaning in life is also the fuel for most capitalist and progressive economies. There are millions of individuals who sacrifice their families, friends, and convictions in the attempt to gain a sense of significance. Accumulating status symbols and material possessions, they seek a position of impor-tance and meaning.

In essence, this deep desire and drive for a sense of importance, significance, and relevance is the cause and the motivator of all human behavior and conflict. This passion for significance knows no boundaries. Rich and poor are victims of its power. King and peasant suffer under its rule. Is this passion for a meaningful life a negative craving? Absolutely not!

This yearning for relevance and significance is evidence of an internal vacuum in the nature of humankind that needs to be filled. This age-old passion is the pursuit of purpose, a relentless reaching for a reason for the gift of life.

You Are Not a Mistake

Have you ever felt like you were a mistake? Have your parents told you they wished you had never been born? Are you a child whose parents have said, "I wish you would have died when you were a baby"?

You may have come into this world as the result of a rape. Your mother may have hated you in the womb because you reminded her of a man she wished to forget. But the fact that you were conceived is more important than how you were conceived. People go around dealing with how things happened, but we should be more concerned with the fact that your conception happened.

What matters is that you are here. You are important. Your very existence means you are somebody special simply because you were born.

Although some parents feel their baby is a mistake, their thoughts are not true. The manner in which a child was conceived may not have been the best, but the child is surely part of a larger, more important plan.

If you were brought up in a nice family with a mother and a father who loved you, you may not understand those who have been put down by their family since the day of their birth. You may not understand how important it is for them to know that they are not mistakes. Be patient with them. Help them to see that every child who comes into this world is special and wanted. You were designed to be somebody special, unique.

The people I have met who are progressing in life and affecting other people's lives—people like Dale Carnegie, a tremendous man who has touched many people's lives, or Robert Schuler, who helped people worldwide to improve their self-esteem—all seem to say the same thing: If you feel good about yourself, you will feel good about other people. In other words, only after you see yourself as a worthwhile person can you appreciate others as worthwhile people.

❖ ◆ ❖

**If you feel good about yourself,
you will feel good about other people.**

❖ ◆ ❖

That's a very important insight because many people do not feel good about themselves. They look at themselves and wonder why they were born; or they doubt that anyone can find any good in them. But remember, each person is valuable and important. Potential has been placed within each one of us. Our potential is not a trial and error experience—we have a predetermined success story.

Your Life Story

I believe each of us has a book—our life stories that have already been written. You may be playing around in the index or you have spent years in the table of contents. Perhaps you are 30 years old and you still don't know the plan for your life. That's playing around on the contents page. You are 30 years old and still wondering what you are supposed to be. You haven't even started yet.

Others have jumped ahead of the plan. Though the design calls for you to be married in Chapter 17, you got married in Chapter 2. You have ignored the things you should have learned and experienced in Chapters 2 through 16, so you would be prepared for marriage in Chapter 17. You have missed out on many experiences and discoveries because you moved ahead of schedule.

Some people are so busy peeking into Chapter 17 they don't have time to live Chapters 2, 3, and 4. Or perhaps you have pulled Chapter 17 into Chapter 2 so that the rest of the book is destroyed. You will never have the opportunity to experience all the chapters if you pull parts of later chapters into the early ones.

Or how about a cell phone? A cell phone has many parts, some visible and some invisible. Among the visible parts of a basic phone are the earpiece and microphone, the key pad, the LCD screen, and the power receptor to plug in your wall charger. Internally, there are wires, a SIM card, a battery, and so on.

If the key pad decides it no longer wants to be a key pad, but prefers to be the LCD screen because it is highly visible, the caller would never reach his party because the phone could not dial the number. Or if the earpiece tries to act like the key pad, the phone would make a call but the caller would not be able to communicate with the other person because the earpiece would not transmit sound.

Like the parts of a phone, each person has a specific place within the overall scheme for the world. Character, nature, gifts, and position are specially designed to accomplish whatever task is purposed for each individual. Frustration results whenever we try to fit into a position too early—or not at all—and we fail to fulfill our potential.

You Are the Author

Starting today, you can write the remainder of your life's story. No matter where you are in life, Chapter 4 or

14, you can make changes to the remaining pages. If you always wanted to be a teacher, take steps to become one! While working as a retail associate you've dreamt about opening your own store, research how to make that happen! If you have always wanted to travel, find a way to use your talents and skills, and go!

Many have often cheated themselves because they don't realize their potential. Why settle for being a doorman when you can own the house? Why settle for cleaning up after dogs when you could open your own dog grooming business? Why settle for being a bank teller when you can be the bank manager? Fulfill your potential by identifying your desires and then planning steps to move in that direction.

Though you might have messed up the first few chapters of your book, you have the chance to write the ending. It probably won't be the best seller the first book was designed to be, but you have the chance to make changes. Self-acceptance is the key to healthy self-esteem. Accept yourself as you are, then transform your weakness, rather than belittling yourself when you make mistakes.

Knock the Limits off Your Life

Knocking the limits off your life gives you the freedom to dream and imagine that all things are possible. Too often we are not willing to believe in ourselves. Everything is possible if we believe. It's not true that everything is possible if we get the idea. Things don't become reality because we have an idea. We have to *believe* in the idea. We have to believe we can do it by committing ourselves to it, abandoning ourselves to it, even if it costs us our lives. That's what it takes to believe.

No one is impressed by our dreams. Most of us never wake up long enough to do anything with our dreams. We may have great dreams for our lives, but we prefer to stay asleep because when we wake up reality says, "OK, let's get to work." It's easier to dream an idea than to work it out. Everything is possible if we abandon ourselves to an idea enough that we are willing to lose our lives for it.

Everything is possible if you abandon yourself to an idea enough that you are willing to lose your life for it.

Thinking is great. But all things are possible when we *believe*. We need to desire a thing enough to want to work for it. The word *desire* is key. Being interested in or attracted to something is not desiring it. To desire means to crave for something at the expense of losing everything.

From Thought to Action

A thought is a silent word, so a word is an exposed thought. Everything in life starts first in thought form. After it's said, it is no longer a thought. It becomes a word.

The next step is an idea. An idea is the concept of the thought—it has moved into a reality. Ideas are potentials.

The third level of operation is what I call imagination. Imagination changes an idea into a plan. If you have an idea, it can come and go. You have many ideas in a day—what to cook, what to wear, what to do. You may decide the night before what you are going to wear in the morning and then wake up with a different idea. Ideas change.

But if an idea develops into an imagination, it means the idea has become a plan. It is still not written or drawn, but it is in your head. Imagination is therefore a plan that is not documented. It is a visual display of your thoughts and ideas.

If you want to be successful in life, take your ideas and turn them into imagination; then take imagination and duplicate it physically. Put it down on paper. Let it become a plan of action.

Many people never get beyond the idea stage. That's sad. They are usually *followers*. The people who get to the imagination stage often talk a lot but they do nothing. They are *dreamers*. But when people take their imagination and put it on paper, you are looking at *visionaries* who could become *missionaries*. Visionaries see great things in their minds. Unfortunately, many visionaries take their visions to the graveyard with them. They had visions, but their visions never made it to mission. When a visionary becomes a *missionary*, you have a man or woman who is going to change the world.

For Instance

If I'm going to create something that will fly, I must first decide that the object's purpose is to fly. Then I have to determine what function and design will allow the object to accomplish that expectation. In other words, I will put into the kite, the helicopter, or the airplane the ability to do what I am asking it to do. My design will include whatever is needed for the object to fly. Because I intended for the object to fly and I built into it the ability to fly, the object can fly. Therefore, purpose produces design, and design predicts potential. From looking at an object's design, you can predict what it is capable of doing.

To back up a step, purpose is also an indication of potential. *If you know the intended purpose for an object, you also know what it can do.* The minute you know that the kite was created to fly, you know that it can fly. Therefore, whatever you were born to do—whatever was purposed for your life—you are equipped with all the ability, talents, gifts, capacities, and potential you need to fulfill it.

Make Plans—Set Goals

Plans are documented imaginations. If you can document an imagination, you've developed a plan for action.

If you are having problems in your life, I mean real problems, you probably don't have a piece of paper on which you have documented your plans for the next five years. If you are disillusioned with life—bored and confused—I can almost guarantee that you don't know what is going on in your life. You're just living from day to day in the absence of a concrete, documented plan by which to live. You've been dealing with the same issues and habits and struggles for years. You slide forward a little only to slide backward again. Whenever things get hard, you start reminiscing about "the good old days" and fall back into habits you had conquered.

If there is no goal in front of you, you'll check the hazardous holes behind you. If there is no vision in front of you to pull you on, you will be dragged back to the path you know well. If your imagination does not become documented, it will soon ferment into vapor and disillusionment.

Let me explain. If you do not have a paper on which you have written a general plan for your life, you may decide something one minute only to change it five minutes later. You will be confused, disoriented, misguided, and frustrated. Progress requires a plan of action. Ideas must be put down if they are to influence the way you live.

Many of us plan our meals for the next week, but we have nothing planned for our lives. The food we eat just goes away—but doesn't touch the future.

Stop. Set your course. Imagine into your future as far as you can.

Chart what you are going to do for the next five months, twelve months, two years. Start imagining what you want to be, what you want to accomplish, where you want to go, who you want to influence. Do this, and then put your plan in a convenient location so you can check your progress, tracking how close you are to your next goal.

You will be amazed how motivating your chart will make you. It will encourage you to move, to work, to look ahead. Don't worry about how you are going to meet all your goals; take one day at a time walking always forward toward them.

You have the capability to change the world. You have the potential to be and do much more than is visible now. Make a plan. Give yourself something to be motivated toward. As you dream, think, imagine, and plan who you want to be, you will begin to see why you were born.

Principles

1. You are worth feeling good about—you are unique.

2. There is a detailed plan for your life.

3. Many plans are waiting to be revealed through you.

4. Develop a plan for your life that fulfills some of the possibilities designed within you.

5. Believe and work those possibilities into existence.

Chapter 5

WHAT *CAN* YOU DO?

*A person cannot discover new oceans unless there is
courage to lose sight of the shore.*

For about two years, our little boy came to me when he was trying to do something and said, "I can't do this." I always responded, "There is nothing named 'can't'." When he came back to me and said, "I don't know how to do it," I always replied, "There's always a way to do everything."

Years ago our young son and I were out in the yard playing ball. I was throwing the ball to him and he kept missing with the bat. Finally he became really upset and said, "I can't do that," to which I replied, "There's nothing named 'can't'." Slowly he repeated after me, "There's nothing named 'can't'." Then I said, "Hold the bat," and I threw the ball. He hit the ball and then said, "There's nothing named 'can't'."

Several days later when I stopped home to drop off our daughter, our son came running and wanted to play basketball. When I said that I had to go back to the office to do some work, he insisted that he wanted to play ball with me right then. When I again replied that I had to go to the office, he said, "There's nothing named 'can't'." Do you see the point? Because he began to think that way at four years of age, the world can expect a winner.

Too often we fail in our efforts because we have been brought up believing that we cannot do some things. The people who change the world are people who have taken *impossible* out of their vocabularies. The men and women who make changes in history are those who come against the odds and tell the odds that it is impossible for the odds to stop them.

**The people who change the world
are those who have taken
impossible out of their vocabularies.**

Inner strength is not a strength that comes once in a while, but a continual ability that is infused into us, I believe, by God. Thus our potential is not limited to doing some things—we can do all things—whatever we believe and desire to do that benefits others. We can do this because the ability to do so is already deposited in us.

Potential is determined by the demands made on it by the creator of it. This is the most amazing thing I have ever discovered about potential. The potential of a thing is determined by the demands made on it by the one who made it. A creator will not call forth from his creation something he did not put into it.

If, for example, the Ford Motor Company wanted to build a car with an engine that was supposed to have a certain degree of horsepower to get up to 200 miles per hour, the engineers would create a car with enough spark plugs and pistons and other things to run at that speed. First they would design it. Then they would build it. Finally they would hire a professional to take it on a test track to clock its speed. Because they designed and built the car to run at 200 miles per hour, they would tell the driver, "Run this car until it hits 200 miles per hour."

Now how can they demand from that car 200 miles per hour? Simple. They built into the car the ability to produce 200 miles per hour. If all other cars can only go 198 miles per hour, they have reason to believe their car will go into a race and win. They are calling forth from the car, or demanding of it, what they created it to produce.

Or let's think about a flight of the spaceship *Challenger*. The people who plan a trip into space decide before the spaceship ever leaves earth when the journey will begin, where the spaceship will go, what the crew will do while in space, how long the trip will last, and where the ship will land. The people who created the spaceship and who trained the astronauts know what the ship and the crew can do. The demands they make are thus consistent with their potential.

Or suppose you want to take a trip. If you want to fly from Nassau to Chicago, you depend upon the expertise and knowledge of others to assure you that you will get there. You may look at the airplane and say, "This thing will never get me to Chicago," but what you think doesn't really matter because you are not the creator of either the airplane or the flight route. The folks who build and maintain the airplane would never require it to make the trip from Nassau to Chicago if they thought the plane lacked the potential to do so. The ticket agent would never schedule you for that airplane if he knew the flight didn't go to Chicago. The potential of a thing is determined by the demands placed upon it by the creator.

Money-Back Guarantee

The same is true of you and your potential. When your dreams, visions, and goals become so real within you that you feel as if you must respond, don't ask whether you can do it, don't argue that you can't. Whatever you believe hard enough, strong enough, and are committed to enough can become reality.

When you buy an appliance, a manual usually comes with it that says: "Read this before you hook it up." It also says: "You've just purchased a television that can do…." You've never seen the television do that before, but the manual says it can and will because the manufacturer made it possible. At the end of the manual, there is usually a little phrase that says: "If there is any defect, return the merchandise to the manufacturer for a free replacement." The manufacturer is guaranteeing the potential of the thing.

When you are on the way to fulfilling your dreams, visions, and goals, you are guaranteed satisfaction because you have the potential already within you!

You Can Do It!

You are capable of producing whatever is demanded of you to reach your potential and destiny. Within a piece of fruit is a tree, a forest even. There is a seed in you too, and that seed has the potential to become a tree—a forest even. It's there, and you need to demand that potential be forthcoming.

Whenever you take on a legitimate responsibility, you will have the ability to meet that responsibility. Whether you use the ability deposited within you is totally up to you. How well you assume the responsibilities you have is not so much a question of how much you do, but rather how much of the available power you use. Chances are that what you are doing is not near what your ability is. What you have accomplished is a joke when compared with what you could accomplish—you are not working enough with the power provided you (emphasis on work).

If You Think It, You Can Do It

Any person who sets a limit on what he or she *can* do, also sets a limit on what he or she *will* do. No one can determine how much you can produce except you. So there is nothing in this world that should stop you from accomplishing and realizing and fulfilling and maximizing your full potential.

If you can conceive it, you can do it.

If you can conceive it, you can do it. It doesn't matter if it has never been done—if you think it, you can do it. Likewise, if you never think it, you can't do it.

Think about the things you've been thinking recently. The fact that you thought them means you can do them. Now don't get me wrong. Thinking doesn't get it done. Thinking implies you can do it. See yourself doing the thing in your thoughts. Make your thought into an idea, and your idea into an imagination. Take that imagination and document it into a plan. Then go to it (of course with the proper rest periods). Put your plan into action. If you thought it, you can do it.

Purpose that is translated into a vision causes things to happen and people to act. This is true because purpose creates vision, vision produces goals, goals permit the development of a plan, and a plan allows for an orderly journey.

Picture for a moment a train station with no tracks. Far in the distance walks a man, coming toward the station. Under his arm he carries wooden planks that he is throwing down before him, building the tracks to the station. The man's goal is to use planks to build a track to the station, which is his desired destination. His vision is the completed track, and his plan is the building of the track by throwing down the planks. Thus, the realization of his goal through the implementation of his plan will take him from his present position to the desired end, so that his vision of the completed track and his purpose of reaching the station are fulfilled.

Goals Are...

Goals are steps toward the attainment of a larger purpose. They create priorities, determine decisions, dictate companions, and predict choices. Together they form the preferred flight plan to the desired destination. Let's examine how this process works by using the image of an airline ticket and the company that stands behind it.

Long before I can book a flight or receive a ticket for a specific destination, some person (who most probably had fulfilled his potential) gave birth to a vision that led to the setting of goals and the development of a plan. A purpose to provide safe air travel in the Western Hemisphere with quality service at affordable prices may have been prompted by too many business trips with extended layovers, canceled flights, and delays caused by mechanical failures. In any case, the founder of an airline fulfilled his potential by considering the possibility of starting a new airline and purposed to do so.

This purpose led to a vision of planes servicing the entire Western Hemisphere, flying from Canada to Argentina and everywhere in-between. In his mind's eye, the soon-to-be airline executive saw his company's insignia on airplanes traveling throughout South America, Central America, the Caribbean, the United States, and Canada. Fueled by his desire to fulfill his potential and purpose and the accompanying vision, the originator of the vision calls in trusted friends and colleagues with whom he shares his thoughts. Others catch his vision and a new airline is founded for the stated purpose of providing safe, economical, quality air service to the Western Hemisphere.

Having a vision and receiving what you have envisioned are two very different things. Guided by their shared vision, the businessman and his friends set goals for the corporation, determining when the flights would begin, which cities would be serviced by the initial service, what the desired profit margin would be, and who would take primary responsibility for each area of operation. As these goals developed into a detailed plan, the person responsible for each facet of the business set goals for their specific areas of operation and developed plans to meet these more specific goals.

Goals Dictate Companions

After the primary and secondary goals had been set and plans developed to meet each objective, the founding committee sought people who could help them accomplish their purpose—whereby also possibly aiding them in fulfilling their potential. Guided by their desire to offer quality service at affordable prices, they hired a research firm to survey the present airline market to see which flight routes are profitable and/or underserviced and a financial consulting group to help raise capital and develop an operating budget. Their aspiration to maintain safe, well-equipped airplanes prompted them to seek a highly experienced airplane mechanic and a test pilot with an impeccable reputation. Together they purchased the planes.

Finally, their ambition to provide quality service led them to hire a personnel director who initially oversaw the development of a standard of service—after researching current airline standards—and later the hiring and management of company employees. Each of these decisions was based on the original purpose to provide safe, affordable, distinctive air service throughout the Western Hemisphere.

Goals Inform Decisions

As each of these people became part of the management team for the new corporation, they were charged with the responsibility of making their decisions based on the collective goals and purposes of the company. No one can pursue his or her own agenda if it detracts from the overall purpose of the plan. The financial consultant, for example, couldn't require the mechanic to purchase an airplane that meets the budget guidelines but is not completely safe. Nor could the personnel director offer salaries and benefits beyond the means of the company. The choices each made to fulfill their individual purpose were influenced by the overall purpose of the company. No one aspect can be sacrificed for the others, or the company's reason for existence would have been jeopardized. Purpose affects everyone's selections.

Goals Predict Choices

Potential and purpose also serves as a guide for determining the best path to a predetermined end. Like a pilot's flight plan, it determines not only the final destination but also the best route on any given day to reach that destination. No pilot leaves the ground without a flight plan. Before he climbs into the cockpit of the plane, he carefully studies the maps, compasses, and other instruments that can help him establish the safest, most direct course to reach the predetermined destination. Then he consults with air traffic control to determine where he needs to adjust his speed or altitude to allow for bad weather or other airplanes. Only after he has completed this task and received a stamped flight plan will he be permitted to guide the plane into the air.

Thus, when the pilot sits in the cockpit and presses the ignition to start the engines, he has with him both the end of the journey and the intended path to reach that end. Unlike a ticket holder, who has only the vision of the final destination, the pilot knows both the final destination and the safest way to reach that airport. The choices he makes on the path to the final destination will always be guided by purpose and the goals related to purpose.

Goals Create Priorities

Even as fulfilling your potential has goals directed by purpose, they also predict choices and create priorities. If the new airline set the first of September as the target date to begin service on the West Coast of the United States, the research firm will not focus their attention on the East Coast. That sphere of service will not be a priority. Likewise, if the goals include the objective of purchasing planes by the first of July, the financial consulting group will have to make the procurement of funds a priority so that this can happen. Purpose informs goals, which define priorities.

Purpose Provides a Measurement of Progress

As each target date on the master plan and the departmental plans passes, the executives are able to determine how well they are progressing toward their goal. If July passes into August, and the mechanic and the pilot have not yet procured any planes, the target date of September for beginning service on the West Coast becomes doubtful. If, however, service on the West Coast begins in mid-August, and additional planes have been purchased to begin service in the Caribbean, the organizing committee knows that they are farther toward fulfilling their purpose than they had expected to be at that point.

Without goals guided by purpose and the resulting vision, they would know that they are making progress, but they wouldn't have any idea whether that progress matches their plans for that specified time. The value of these goal-informed evaluations cannot be overemphasized because life without specific, measurable objectives is vague and haphazard.

Obviously this description of the process of beginning a new airline is very simplistic, but I think it provides a pattern for you to understand about a person—persons—fulfilling his potential. Placing yourself in the position to make your dreams come true is the first step to making known your purpose, which enhances all of life, enabling a decisive, intentional perspective.

Fundamentals

I believe there are certain characteristics that people must understand before they can understand their potential. Realizing these basic human concepts is something that you *can* do to open doors that you never knew were locked against you. Some of these fundamentals may seem very obvious and simple to you, but they are very important to consider carefully before we move on.

Love. Love isn't a decision you make, because you already have it. That's why you can love your enemies. You can never have too much love. Spread it around. Accept it.

Self-control. Self-control is essential when growing relationships, maintaining friendships, and advancing in your journey toward your destiny. Self-control is the sign of a mature person, ready to be an example for others.

Patience. Patience is a virtue that few have much of. In an instant-message age, people are not inclined to be patient. Absorb this virtue and you will become admired for it.

Peace. The kind of inner peace you enjoy when you accept yourself as a treasure will keep you comforted no matter the toil or turmoil going on around you.

Courage. What challenge do you face? What are you afraid of? Just remember, fear is necessary for courage to exist. Courage can only be manifested in the presence of fear. So use fear to exercise your courage.

When you face difficulties, your answer is not in your counselor or the books you read. These can be helpful for input, but the answer is in you. Lean on the fundamentals and you will never go wrong.

You Are More Than You or Others Expect

One morning I said to my little boy as he ran into the room and jumped on me, "You know, I'm holding in my hands all you haven't been yet." Although he didn't understand much of what I was saying, I was thinking about the vast amount of potential that lay within him just waiting to be used.

Potential is like that. It's all you can be and become that you haven't yet experienced. Think about it. Potential is all you are capable of being or doing or reaching. You haven't done it yet, but you *can* do it.

You Can Overcome Any Habit

You can overcome every habit. You are not involved in a hopeless fight. Oh, hear me if you are suffering a habit. You *can* beat it.

Maybe you have resolved that you are hooked for life. That's a lie. You have authority over that habit. Don't walk around with the hopeless idea: "I'll always be an addict. I'll always be an alcoholic. I'll always be like this."

Within you is the ability to dominate everything on earth. It is there. It is in you. The problem isn't that you can't control your habit; the problem is that you won't. People say: "I know I shouldn't be doing this." In reality that means: "I don't want to do this. Something is wrong with this but I can't help myself."

I have news for you—good news. It's more "I haven't decided to stop doing this," than "I shouldn't be doing this."

Stop being ruled by cocaine or marijuana. Don't be the victim of alcohol and money. They are all but leaves from the trees that we are supposed to be dominating. Don't allow yourself to be at the beck and call of a little bottle that says: "Come here…come drink me." Don't allow yourself to be controlled by leaves from Colombia. The only way to escape these and other dominating habits is to understand your purpose for being. You are not to be dominated by sex or chemicals. You were not created to be controlled by anything. *You* are to control the earth.

You Are the Cream of the Crop

You are so much more than others expect from you. You are so much more than you expect from yourself. You are special, elite, the cream of the crop. Under all the junk that you may have allowed to accumulate, there is a gem ready to be polished and displayed. Beneath your unrighteous behavior there is a righteous person who wants to do the right thing. Keep striving to unclog that well. Keep trying to expose the real you.

When you wake up tomorrow morning, stretch, look in the mirror, and say: "You successful thing you." No matter what kind of bum day is planned for you, you can decide in the morning that it's going to be a successful one. Why? Because if you believe, it is possible the day will be good. It is possible to rejoice every day. Go ahead. Stretch. Look at the success that is just waiting to happen.

What a blessing it is to know that we can wake up tomorrow morning and have a fresh start. But too often we wake up and say: "Oh, God. It's Monday." Come on, let's go out there and give people a firm handshake, an honest compliment, and a big smile! You will be amazed at the reactions you will receive. Your attitude is something you *can* do something about.

Don't Let the World Determine Your Potential

We have allowed the world around us to determine our potential. Teachers say to students: "You are a C student." The student then goes around believing that, and he becomes an average student for the rest of his life—an average person even. He becomes an average husband.

She becomes an average wife. We become average parents of average children with average attitudes and IQs. And when we turn out to be average, our parents say: "Well, honey, you have my genes." No. They received your *attitude* that was transmitted to you from that teacher.

You need to shake off what people call IQs. Do you know what IQ means? Intelligence Quotient—it's what people believe your degree of intelligence is based upon some tests you take. These tests measure your motor skills, thinking ability, cognitive ability, reading ability, math ability, etc. Then based on these tests they say, "You are a D student. You are a D person." You haven't even grown up yet, and they are telling you what you are going to be and do! They don't know what you are going to do.

Unfortunately, people believe what they are told based on those tests. There are thousands of examples in history of men and women who were put off and cast out as misfits. Later they turned out to be some of the world's greatest leaders. We must be careful when we start assigning Intelligence Quotients to people. Your potential has nothing to do with those tests.

Only a Page

I recently attended a function to honor a gentleman in our community—a tremendous man. Several people gave speeches about him, talking about his many accomplishments. As I sat there I thought, *Wow! If you only knew.*

A booklet on the table listed all the things he had accomplished. As I looked at it I thought, *Is that all—half a page? There's a book on that man but here he only has a page.*

Rest, Not Retirement

There are times when we get tired of our jobs. In fact, we get so tired that we look forward to retirement. And when we get to that age, we just want to retire—we want to stop working permanently. But I believe this is wrong—wrong thinking. We should be thinking rest, not retirement. Why? Because we need to keep creating and developing and dominating and ruling for as long as possible. The wealth of your potential is so rich it requires a lifetime and beyond to bring it all out.

Try to do as much now as you can. Pack as much as you can into the 70 to 100 years you have here. Go for it. Go for a hunk of gold. Go for the mountain that has the gold in it. Go for the whole thing. Because if you can think it, you can do it.

Principles

1. The potential of a thing is related to its source.

2. Your potential is greater than you can ever imagine.

3. Potential is determined by the demands made on it by its creator.

4. If you can think it, you can do it.

5. Your potential is everything you need to dominate any bad habit or addiction.

6. The wealth of your potential is so rich it requires a lifetime to bring it all out.

Chapter 6

CHALLENGE YOUR ABILITY

Your ability needs responsibility to expose its possibilities.
Do what you can with what you have where you are.
—Theodore Roosevelt

The people who are blessings to humanity are usually men and women who decide there is more to them than what other people have said. People who bless the world are people who believe there is an ability inside them to accomplish something that has never been done. Though they may not know exactly what they can do, they try because they believe they can accomplish something.

How High Can You Jump?

I remember the day I discovered that I could jump really high—about eight feet high. Now, I can't jump that high intentionally, but I did it once when I was a little boy.

There was a lady who lived behind our house from whose fruit trees we would occasionally help ourselves and feast upon. When we were little kids, we would crawl under the fence. One day while I was on her side of the fence, her very vicious dog suddenly appeared. I had just touched down after climbing the fruit tree. As I carefully considered the distance between the fence, the dog, and myself, I knew I had to make a run for it. I ran toward the fence with the dog close behind me. As the fence came closer and closer, all I could say was "Oh God, I'm dead." All I could think was, *Jump!* As I left the ground, my heart was pounding and my chest felt like an arcade full of shouting people. I was so afraid! When I landed, I was safely on the other side of the fence.

When I turned around and looked at the dog, he was barking angrily because he couldn't get over the fence. I just thought, *Yea, good for you.* Suddenly I became very proud because I had gotten away from him. But when I started to realize what I had done, I looked at the fence and thought, *How did I do that?*

I thank God for that dog. He was a blessing in my life. I never jumped that high before, and I never have since, but at least I know that I did it. I discovered that day there is a lot more potential in me than I realized.

The same is true for you. You aren't doing more because no one has challenged you. I want to take you from the realm of waiting for people to challenge you and encourage you to challenge yourself. Don't wait for a dog to teach you how to jump. Jump by your own challenge. Don't just look at life and say, "Well, I'm going to wait until a demand is made on me and then I will produce." Make a demand on yourself. Say to yourself, "Look, I am going to become the best in this area no matter what people have done before me." Then go after that. You will accomplish it if you set out to do it.

Tell Me to Come

That reminds me of a young fisherman who decided, "I'm going to take a chance and try to walk on water." One night as he and his friends were crossing a lake, it was hard rowing. They were being tossed about by the waves because the wind was against them. As they struggled, a man came toward them, walking on the water. In fear they cried out, "It's a ghost." Only when He spoke to them did they recognize Him. The young fisherman said, "If it's You, tell me to come to you on the water." The Man said "Come!" The young fisherman had the guts to respond.

I believe all those men in the boat could have walked on water. The potential was in them even as it was in the one who stepped out. But only he succeeded, because only he had the guts to say, "If You challenge me, I'll take Your challenge." Although we may laugh or criticize him for sinking after a few steps, none of us has ever walked on water.

—— ✦ ✦ ✦ ——

**Don't die without maximizing
your abilities—that's irresponsible.**

—— ✦ ✦ ✦ ——

We need to be willing to say, "Tell me something to do. Give me something to challenge my potential." Men and women who are assets to the world and bring change for the better are those who give their potential something to maximize. Give your ability a responsibility that would change the world. There is a wealth of ability in you, but you haven't given it any responsibility.

Don't die without maximizing your ability—that's irresponsible. You have no right to die with all that latent potential just waiting to be shared.

Don't Wait to Be Challenged

You have a skill or ability the world needs. Miracles happen when we give our potential responsibility. Don't allow the things within you to die with you because you did not challenge them. The seed of potential is planted within you. You were made according to the potential principle—like the rest of creation. Don't waste that gift. Give your potential some responsibility.

One of humankind's greatest struggles is determining what is most important in life. Each of us must at some point decide what we are living for if our lives are to have focus and a sense of purpose and fulfillment. Compounding the challenge is the fact that we live in a culture that regards truth as relative and life as meaningless. If life is an evolutionary accident, then there is no such thing as absolute truth or morality and no high and exalted purpose for human existence. Consequently, many people give up on life and, if they don't commit suicide first, retreat into a mindset of cynicism, hopelessness, and despair.

At the same time, there are many people who yearn for a simpler life free of the stress, struggles, and hectic pace of our high-speed, high-tech, multiple-option, anything-goes society. With so many choices, how do you choose the best, the most important? How do you make sure that you are spending your life on the things that really count?

Over the last 30 years or so my life has become very simple. That does not mean I am not busy. My life is quite full. I frequently travel internationally and rarely have an empty schedule. Yet, in spite of my "busyness," my life is simple because I have spent the last three decades learning to live according to priorities I have set for myself.

Beat the Odds

Men and women who make changes in history are those who have come against the odds and told the odds it is impossible for the odds to stop them. Don't throw yourself away; don't let anyone else throw you away because you are up against some odds.

◆ ◆ ◆

**You have a skill or ability
the world needs.**

◆ ◆ ◆

The minute we see someone in a wheelchair, something happens to us. Many of us think the person is half a person. We almost treat him as if we apologize for his condition. We look at a person who is blind, who has a withered hand, who walks with a limp, who has only one arm as though they are less than us. We limit their potential to the wheelchair or the limp or the missing hand or the short arm. We reduce everybody to their physical bodies. You are not your body. Some of the greatest minds in the world are in wheelchairs.

I think about President Franklin D. Roosevelt in a wheelchair. Did you ever think an invalid could be the president of one of the greatest nations on earth? I think of a young boy I read about. A great mathematician, who suffered from a disease that destroyed his bones. He just sort of faded away. He looked ugly compared to what we call beauty. His glasses were falling off to the side because his face was caving in. His nose was almost gone. His teeth were all messed up. His whole body was warped. He couldn't write. Yet he could figure the greatest mathematical calculations of the time. Professors went to his home, sat at his desk, and wrote everything he said. They developed mathematical books for the universities from this brain in the chair. His illness had not destroyed his potential. His genius is not affected by his physical appearance. He was a young man determined to beat the odds by using all the formulas and potential stored within him.

Suppose you end up in a wheelchair next year with all the brains you have right now. Will you quit? Is your dream related to your body? Don't say no too fast. You may just quit and get totally depressed and sad. You might say, "Oh, life didn't work out for me," and you'd allow all the dreams you have right now to die in the chair. You'd simply quit.

---◆◆◇---

Suppose you end up in a wheelchair
with all the brains you have right now.
Would you give up on life?

---◆◆◇---

I think about Mr. Penney who founded the retail store, JC Penney. Born an orphan (he didn't even know who his parents were), he refused to be like many people I know who sit around and say: "Everybody treats me badly. No one cares for me. I guess I ought to go on drugs and just blow it." Penney decided that there was a food store in him and a clothing store and a department store. So he acquired his first job working in a store packing bags. I can almost hear him thinking as he packed bags one day: *One of these days they're going to pack these for me.* Like many others who have given much to humankind, Penney believed that he had the ability to make something of his life. And now we go and spend money buying things at his JC Penney stores.

Don't give up because you are physically handicapped. Don't give up if you are facing great odds. Your potential is not determined by whether you can see the fine print of a book, walk across the street, or lift heavy objects with one hand. Your potential is not destroyed because your mother is an alcoholic, your father's a junkie, or you have no parents at all. There are many people in wheelchairs who have given up. There are many people who come from the wrong side of town or a bad family situation who have given up. Don't be one of them. Beat the odds.

Shortcuts Don't Work

Ben Johnson is an athlete from Canada who set many world records. In 1987 he set the world record in the one hundred yard dash at 9.83 seconds. In 1988 he broke his own record, winning the race in 9.79. But it is difficult to be correct in calling that a world record because the last record set was not the record of Ben Johnson. It was the record of a steroid pill. That record belongs to Ben Johnson plus the chemicals.

We will never know Ben Johnson's potential as far as running the one hundred yard dash is concerned. Could he have run one hundred yards in 9.79 seconds without the chemical? Possibly, but we will never know because Ben Johnson negated his potential by trying a shortcut. There was no reason for his shortcut. He had a world record. He had his name in history, and it was a good name. How sad to destroy a good name by a little bit of chemical.

I picked up a magazine on an airplane in which there was an advertisement, "Would you like a doctorate degree? Call us." I often read that advertisement and wonder how many have called. If I did not realize that you cannot get something for nothing, I probably would have called them. Many have. There are people out there with doctorate degrees, or with doctorate letters in front of their names, who will never know their potential. They didn't allow themselves the chance to see what they could really do. They have the degrees, but they didn't fulfill the requirements.

There are no shortcuts to developing your potential. You will never know what you might have achieved if you use a crutch to get there. You'll never know what you may have learned if you get a degree without fulfilling the requirements. You will never know what you can do if you attempt to obtain it by a shortcut. Shortcuts negate potential. They destroy the possibilities planted within you.

Demand Something of Your Potential

Potential must be exercised to be fulfilled. Demands must be made on potential if it is to be released and fulfilled. You have potential. Unless you make demands on it, you will die with it. Unless you venture to try things you've never done before, you'll never experience the wealth that lives within you. Decide today, "I'm going to do something I've never done before...I'm going to get a promotion this year in my job." If you have a business, resolve to cut the overhead and increase service. Give your potential some demands. It needs to be maximized and challenged.

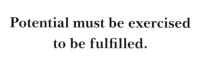

**Potential must be exercised
to be fulfilled.**

The greatest works in the world will be done by people who don't care who gets the credit. I don't want to be famous, I just want to be faithful. I don't want to be well-known, I want to be well-used. I don't want to be powerful, I want to be potent. Success requires striking out on new paths instead of traveling those that are well-worn. As attributed to Albert Einstein, "Genius is one percent inspiration and ninety-nine percent perspiration." There are many people with great ideas, but they have no desire to try. There are four steps to the accomplishment of your dream: Prepare practically. Plan purposefully. Proceed positively. Pursue persistently. Remember, failure is the path of least persistence.

Don't Be Afraid to Try

People can't climb beyond the limitations they have placed on themselves. Success is never final—failure is never fatal. It is courage that counts—courage and the willingness to move on. A great deal of talent is lost to the world for want of a little courage. Every day sends to the grave obscure people whom fear and timidity have prevented from making their first attempt to do something. Never tell a person that something can't be done, because that person may hold the key to curing a disease, teaching a child to read, inventing a new energy source.

***

**Success is never final—
failure is never fatal.**

***

The poorest of people are people without dreams. Don't be so afraid of failure that you refuse to try. Demand something of yourself. Failure is only an incident. There's more than the failure—there's success deep behind that failure. Failure is the opportunity to more intelligently begin again. When you fail, that is a great chance to start again. Learn from it and move on. Don't be paralyzed by the failure.

One good thing about failure is that it is proof that you tried. The greatest mistake you can make is to be afraid of making one. People who do nothing in life are usually people who do nothing. People who don't make mistakes in life are usually people who didn't have a chance to make any because they never tried.

Challenge your potential. Demand things of yourself that are beyond what you have already done. Expect more from yourself than the accomplishments that are easily within your reach. What you have is not all you are. You are the one who limits your potential. It is better to attempt a thing and fail, than to never try and not know you could succeed.

Principles

1. Believe there is potential in you to accomplish something worthwhile.

2. Unless you use your potential, you will never realize how much ability is inside you.

3. Jump by your own challenge. Don't wait for someone to challenge you.

4. Don't let the odds that are against you stop you from fulfilling your potential.

5. Shortcuts negate your ability.

6. Don't be so afraid of failure that you refuse to try.

Chapter 7

Your Potential's Purpose

The potency of your potential
requires eternal life to be realized.

Nothing is more tragic than a life without purpose. Why is purpose so important? Purpose is the source of priorities. Defining our life's priorities is extremely difficult unless we first discover and define our purpose. Purpose is defined as the original reason and intent for the creation of a thing. Therefore, purpose is the source of meaning and significance for all created things.

If purpose is not known, priorities cannot be established and nothing significant or worthwhile in life can be accomplished. In essence, if you don't know why you are on planet Earth and posses a clear sense of purpose and destiny, the demand for priorities is low or nonexistent. The truth is, if you don't know where you are going, any road will take you there. Life is daily and constantly demanding of our time, energy, talent, attention, and focus. Therefore, to effectively manage the everyday demands, we must know what our priorities are. No matter what we think about life, we have to live it every day and give an account of our management.

I believe the greatest challenge in life is the daily demand to choose between competing alternatives that consume our lives. If we do not have clear and correct priorities in our lives and know what we should be doing, our lives will be an exercise in futility. The absence of priority is dangerous and detrimental.

Absence of priority results, first of all, in the *wasting of time and energy*. If you're not doing the right thing at the right time, that means you are doing the wrong thing at the wrong time. But you expend the same time and energy either way. Time and energy, once spent, are gone forever. They cannot be replaced.

When priority is absent, you become *busy on the wrong things*. If you don't know what the right things are, you will end up focusing on the wrong things. These "wrong things" may not be bad or evil in themselves; they are just wrong for *you* because they will distract you from pursuing your life purpose.

People without priority spend their time *doing the unnecessary*. If you think about it, most of what we do on a daily basis is not really necessary. We spend most of our time sweating, fretting, and laboring over issues that, in the eternal scheme of things, are pointless. And in the meantime, the things that really matter go undone.

In a similar way, absence of priority causes people to *major on the unimportant*. If you have no priority, you end up majoring on the minors. For some reason most of us are easily distracted or enticed away from focusing on the most important matters in life to concentrate instead on peripheral issues. Priority helps sharpen our vision so we can focus on the most important things. Without it, we have no sense of direction and are apt to pursue whatever suits our fancy at the time.

Consequently, the absence of priority results in *preoccupation with the unimportant*. Not only do we focus on the unimportant, we become preoccupied with it. We think about it, debate it, discuss it, argue about it, and have conferences on it until, by default, it becomes a de facto priority for us. But even then, it is still the *wrong* priority.

Preoccupation leads to investment, so absence of priority causes us to *invest in the less valuable*. Who would invest in something that could produce only a 10-fold return instead of something that guarantees a 100-fold return? We all invest our time, energy, and money on those things that we deem most important and of greatest value. What if we're wrong? Unless we know what is truly important, it is impossible for us to invest wisely. So the end result of the absence of priority is wasted resources.

Another consequence of absent priority is *ineffective activity*. No matter how busy you are or how much you believe you are accomplishing, if you are focused on the wrong thing all your activity will count for nothing in the end. You will be ineffective because you did not do what you were supposed to do.

The first key to effectiveness is to be sure you are doing the right thing. Then invest your time, attention, energy, and resources to doing it well. Otherwise, no matter how hard you work or how hard you try, you will not succeed.

One of the most serious consequences of absent priority is that it leads to the *abuse of gifts and talents*. If you use your talent to do something that you are not supposed to do, you have wasted your talent, even if you use it well. Some of the most gifted and talented people in the world use their abilities in ways never intended, pursuing selfish desires, indulging in lust and immorality, encouraging sensuality, and promoting values that are destructive to family and society. Having talent is one thing, but knowing how to make it serve the top priority in your life is a different story. Imagine being a gifted speaker proclaiming the wrong message or a talented singer singing the wrong song. It happens every day, and it is a tragedy.

People with no priority in life *forfeit purpose*. Everybody has a purpose in life but most people, sadly, never discover it. Without priority in your life you will never understand your purpose and if you do not understand your purpose you will not pursue it. If you are not pursuing the purpose you were born for, then you are pursuing the wrong thing. Even if you succeed in your pursuit you have still failed because you have not fulfilled your potential. So, absence of priority will forfeit your purpose for living.

Finally, absence of priority results in *failure*. No matter how successful you are in what you do, if you are not doing the most important thing, the thing that you are supposed to be doing, you are failing. Busy activity, sweat, and hard work are important as long as you are focused on the right assignment. However, they can never substitute for correct priority. Priorities are like river banks; they control the flow of life.

Tapping Our Potential

As we discuss the awesome task of tapping our true and full potential, it is essential that we come to appreciate how important each one of us is and how special we are, especially to each other. If you were aware of how much power and worth you have, the first thing that would be affected would be your attitude toward yourself.

Many of us have a difficult time projecting a good attitude toward others because we feel badly about ourselves. Great positive thinkers and personal motivators, along with psychologists, all agree that if you feel good about yourself, then your attitude toward others will be influenced by that attitude. However, for many positive-thinking programs, this is simply an attempt to convince one's self by mental assent that you are of value and worth. It's an attempt to convince you of something you don't believe.

On the contrary, what we are discussing here is something different. We are talking about a fact grounded in truth and reality. I believe that your worth, value, and potential have all been given by God, and there is no formula, test, or scheme to measure the full extent of these qualities and abilities.

Therefore I would like to reiterate some principles and concepts that were discussed in earlier chapters. It is essential that you understand these if you are going to tap into your true and full potential.

Potential's Purpose

Wherever something comes from determines the potential it has. The degree or potency of that potential can be measured by the demands made on it by the one who made it. Therefore, the potential or ability of a thing is determined by the purpose for which the creator, manufacturer, or maker made it.

Every product is designed and engineered by the manufacturer to fulfill its purpose. Therefore its potential is built in. The purpose establishes the demands to be placed on the product, and the demands determine its potential.

This principle is evidenced by all manufacturers who enclose a manual with their product detailing the expected performance and potential of their product. The manufacturer wants you to read the manual before using the product so you know what demands to make on the product. They are confident you can make those demands because they have already built into the product the necessary components to fulfill the demands. The potential of a thing is therefore not determined by opinions, assumptions, or prejudices, but only by the demands placed on it by the one who made it.

Your true ability and potential should not be measured by the limitations of an academic test or an Intelligence Quotient score. Nor should it be determined by the social, cultural, economic, and educational "norms" of your society. Society did not create you. You are not a product of your culture. You are not the offspring of your economy. You were not created by the Department of Education. Therefore, none of these has the right to determine how much potential you really possess. I believe that God created all humankind and that He built into each of us unlimited potential.

Principle

The potential of a thing is determined by the demands made on it by the one who made it.

What Are the Limits of Your Potential?

It seems to me that the people who change the world and significantly impact humanity are those who have discovered the limitless nature of their potential. They are people who decided to take the word *impossible* out of their vocabularies. If you are going to realize and maximize your full potential, you will have to understand the true nature of your potential.

This process-principle introduces us to additional principles that we must understand if we are to fully appreciate the nature of our potential. These principles are evidenced in nature and are scientifically sound. They are as follows:

1. Wherever something came from, it is composed of the same material substance as where it came from. It is a composite of its source.

2. Wherever something came from, it has to be sustained and maintained by where it came from.

3. The potential of a thing cannot be fulfilled without being related to its source.

These principles are clearly demonstrated in nature. The plants came from the earth and they must remain related (attached) to the earth in order to live and be fruitful. The stars came from the gasses in space and must therefore remain in space in order to remain effective.

The fish came from the water and must remain related (submerged) in water in order to live. The animals are products of the soil and must remain related (feed on) soil (dirt) products in order to live.

The key to knowing your true potential is to know your Source. You will never understand, realize, or maximize your true and full potential without a relationship with your Source.

Exploring the Potential of Our Triune Selves—Body, Soul, and Spirit

I believe that humans are triune beings consisting of three distinct yet intricately related dimensions. Each dimension is designed to fulfill a specific purpose. Each realm is designed with the potential to maximize its function and fulfill its intended purpose. Let us now take a closer look at each part of humanity and explore the untapped potential that lies buried there.

The Potential of the Body

In pursuit of knowledge about our world and environment (through the disciplines of science), we explore the various aspects of creation and reach the general conclusion that the magnificent mystery of the human body still stands at the apex of all natural forms of creation. For decades, specialists have dedicated their lives to the study of the physiological potential of the human body—its ability to handle pressure; to adjust itself to varying environmental changes; to defend itself against disease, danger, or threat; to maintain its stamina under physical exertion. Yet, despite humankind's technological advancements and scientific explorations of this masterpiece of creation, scientists continue to admit that they have limited knowledge concerning the potential of this mechanism of precision we call the human body.

The human body has been described as 80 percent water (fluid), with a degree of calcium, fiber, and tissue. But to fully appreciate the true potential of the human body, we must understand the purpose for its creation.

The Purpose of the Body

I believe that the human body was specifically designed to relate to and live in the earth or physical realm—not the spiritual or supernatural world. It is essential, then, that we do not judge our true potential by the abilities or limitations of our physical bodies. For this reason, our five senses are specifically designed to be adjoined to our natural environment. Our powers of sight, touch, hearing, smell, and taste are all related to the natural, physical world. The potential of our bodies is therefore governed by its physical capabilities. But we are not to be controlled or limited by our physical bodies. You were not created to be intimidated by your environment.

From the Inside Out

We were designed to live from the inside to the outside—from our spirits to our bodies. We are to be led by our spirits, not driven by our environments. It is my belief that we were intended to live through spiritual discernment, not physical senses. This way of living is the difference between people who can walk calmly through tragic circumstances while others are screaming in despair.

If we become victims of our souls (mind, will, emotions) and our bodies (five senses), there is no peace, no control. Being governed by our external environments gives our five senses control of our existence, and chaos is the result.

Measuring our lives, worth, and value by our environments gives birth to humanistic philosophy. In reality, the body and its sensual capacity is the measure of reality in this modern-day world. When we started living and interpreting our existence according to information gained through the senses of our bodies, instead of revelation received through our spirits, we placed our bodies in positions they had not been designed to occupy. This change has caused us to *limit* our potential ability to the *very limited* capabilities of our senses and our physical bodies.

Dignified Dirt

No matter how majestic and wonderful the human body is, we must be careful to remember the reality of its composition. According to the Bible it was formed from the dust of the ground. According to scientists, it is composed of natural elements including water, oxygen, carbon, calcium, and nitrogen. If the physical body is related to the earth, it must be sustained and maintained by the earth. The body must feed on soil (dirt) in order to live (plants, animals, fish, etc.). We must, therefore, understand that our bodies—though they have tremendous potentials, powers, capabilities, and values—must never become the full measure of our potential.

Physical Handicap—Myth or Master

There are millions of physically handicapped individuals who, because of their society's concept of potential, have resigned themselves to a life of self-pity, depression, and isolation. There are many who have confused their bodies with their true selves. They have mistaken the "house" for the "resident."

But history gives ample evidence of thousands who have freed themselves of the myth that their bodies should dictate their true potential. They have defied the limitations of their "dirt houses" and soared to the unlimited heights of their souls' and spirits' potential. Many have turned their wheelchairs into the cockpits of jetliners as they explored the heights of their capabilities. Others have used their walking canes to pole vault them into positions that changed the world. Some transformed their world of silence to produce sounds that many are enjoying today.

Still others have used their blindness to see beyond the physical. They have captured sights others long to see.

Helen Keller refused to be blinded by others' opinions of her ability—she changed the attitude of the world. Sir Winston Churchill refused to be muted by his speech impediment and physical handicap—while a member of the British Parliament and later the Prime Minister of Britain, he delivered some of history's most life-changing orations.

What is your handicap? Is it a wheelchair, a bed, a walker, the socio-economic status of your family, or the color of your skin? Is it the ghetto, your parents' lifestyle, the level of your education, or a terminal illness? Are you disabled by divorce, the absence of your parents, incest, or child abuse? Are you blind or deaf? Do you have a speech impediment or poor self-esteem? Whatever your perceived handicap may be, you must never allow your true potential to become a victim of the limitations of your physical body or your environment. Reach beyond your grasp. Your body is not your full potential.

❖ ❖ ❖

Reach beyond your grasp.
Your body is not your full potential.

❖ ❖ ❖

I encourage you to develop and maintain a correct attitude toward your body. Learn to keep your body clean and healthy. You are the steward of this precious earthly vessel. Its maintenance and effective operation are your responsibility. Like any essential equipment, your body needs regular checkups, proper amounts of fuel (food), periods of recuperation and recreation (rest, sleep, and fasting), and invigorating exercise. But do not allow your body to become the dictator of your potential. You are not your body.

Please note that the previous reference describes the physical body as being in a state of daily disintegration. If we determine our potential by the condition of our bodies— whether we are handicapped or relatively healthy and fit—we are still relying on a premise that is constantly dissolving. You and I must not allow any physical impediment or the natural aging process to immobilize the potential that lies within us.

You must refuse to limit your true potential by the limitations of your physical body.

The Potential of the Soul

Some years ago a famous pop singer sang a song entitled "I'm a Soul Man." That title became a common phrase throughout the Western world. I suspect he was referring to the cultural-ethnic orientation of the Afro-American artistic expression. But the statement communicates both a statement of truth and a myth. As discussed earlier, the soul is the triunity of the mind, the will, and the emotions. The soul was created for the purpose of receiving revelation from the spirit-self to communicate it to the body and information from the physical senses to transmit it to the spirit-self.

In essence, the soul was designed to be the "servant" of the spirit-self, and the body was designed to be the "servant" of the soul. Humanity is a spirit, lives in a body, and possesses a soul.

**Humanity is a spirit, lives in
a body, and possesses a soul.**

The soul became a victim of his body and the physical senses. When revelation from the spirit-self was replaced by information from the physical senses, humankind became a victim of the environment with education as the primary goal. In fact, we were reduced to a "soul man." Never allow a teacher's opinion, or the score on an academic test, or the fact that you didn't complete your formal education to dictate the magnitude of your potential. The exercise of the soul can make you smart, but not wise. Depend on the limitless potential that is stored in your spirit to boost you into the next realm of success!

The Potential of Your Spirit

The measure of your true potential is your spirit. When we live from the inside—from the spirit self—we live knowing that there is more to us tomorrow than what there is of us today. Without that relationship, you are limited to the potential of your soul and your body.

An important verse in the Bible that was written to the Romans before their great fall, *"Those who live according to the sinful nature have their minds set on what that nature desires; but those who live in accordance with the Spirit have their minds set on what the Spirit desires"* (Rom. 8:5). I agree completely. Nature and natural desires are almost always selfish, self-centered, and destructive. The supernatural spirit within, though, focuses on the betterment of self and others.

There are things concerning you that your soul can never receive, because it cannot discern them. Yet your spirit has the ability and knows your potential that will astonish you and your family. Whether you are young or old, rich or poor, black or white, a college graduate or a high-school dropout, you are still a treasure of potential.

The measure of your true potential can only be tapped by living from the inside out—by lifting that cap off the well. Go after the deep things that are related to your potential; go as deep as possible. Decide to discover your true potential.

Principles

1. The key to knowing your true potential is to know your Source.

2. Humankind is a triune being: body, soul, and spirit.

3. Your spirit is intended to relate to God, the soul to the mental realm, and the body to the physical environment.

4. Your body is not the measure of your true potential.

5. Your soul (mind, will, and emotions) is not the measure of your true potential.

6. The measure of your true potential is your spirit.

Chapter 8

Ten Keys to Fulfilling Your True Potential

What lies behind us and what lies before us are tiny matters, compared to what lies within us.
—Oliver Wendell Holmes

We are complexly designed, tremendously built, intricately put-together pieces of equipment. But we don't know all that we can do. We can't even imagine the full extent of our potential.

When we examine this piece of equipment, instead of marveling at its construction, accepting its uniqueness, and appreciating the potential within, we think it should be fixed in one way or another. We sometimes take it to a second-rate, second-class, unskilled technician who muddles the job with insincere suggestions and uncaring comments.

Sometimes we even submit our specialized equipment and product to an unauthorized dealer with no genuine parts. Though someone else has tried to fix us and has messed us up, we can start all over again—today, right now. We can rebuild and remake ourselves. We know us better than anybody else—only we can uncap the well that is holding back our true potential.

You were created to rule over all the earth and everything that creeps in it. You won't dream or imagine anything that isn't already built into you to produce or achieve. Thus, if the earth in any way is dominating you, you are malfunctioning. You were not created to give in to cigarettes or submit to alcohol. You were not created to be controlled by drugs, sex, money, power, or greed. If any of these are governing you, you are living below your privilege. You have the ability to dominate the earth—believe it. Everything in the earth must be under your subjection, not mastering you.

—◆ ◆ ◆—

**You have the ability to imagine
and plan to do anything.**

—◆ ◆ ◆—

You have the ability to imagine and plan and bring into being anything you desire. If you decide to do something, and you believe in it hard enough and commit yourself to work for it long enough, nothing in the universe can stop you. If you want to do anything, you can do it. Only if you lack the commitment to follow after your dream will your dream remain unfinished. The potential to do and plan anything is in you—if you will believe and persevere.

Not only are you able to plan, but you also have the ability to believe something that seems impossible and actually make it possible. If you can abandon yourself to an idea and sacrifice all you have for that idea, it's possible for that idea to come to pass. You have the potential to influence physical and spiritual matter.

**You have the potential to believe
impossibilities into possibilities.**

You have the power to influence things in both the physical and spiritual realms. You may never have imagined that you possess that kind of power. But you do.

You have a blank check—but there is one condition on the cashing of that check: You must believe in yourself, your potential, your commitment to make your dreams come true and accomplish your goals. Remember, you won't aspire to anything that you haven't been already wired to do.

Realize the vastness of your potential. If you receive a vision or dream of an assignment, be confident that you already have the ability to fulfill it. Along with the demand always comes the capability to meet that demand. But remember: only you can fulfill and maximize your true potential.

Remember too that unwise, greedy, and selfish decisions and choices clog up your potential. Disobedience may have stunted your capacity for growth. But you can always unclog the well by admitting your mistake, changing your attitude, and choosing to make the right decisions. You need to know who you are and the fullness of your potential. You can reopen the capacity of the best of who you are and unclog your true self.

Forgive yourself, ask forgiveness of others, and you will live with hope and peace in your heart. In a plugged-up state, you can't begin to touch your true ability. Only after you start living a good and righteous life can you start the journey of fulfilling all the potential planted within you before you were born.

It is my earnest desire that you will realize the awesome wealth of potential residing in you. These following ten keys will unlock that cap to your well that is just waiting to overflow into years of success and accomplishments!

Some Fundamental Keys

The key to life promotions and fulfillment is to keep our pipeline clear of any obstructions. This means working hard to keep ourselves in line and avoiding anything that will move us out of position. Don't lie, don't cheat, don't curse, and don't want what someone else has. Let go of anger, envy, and jealousy. Be quick to forgive and always ready to extend mercy. Treat everyone with kindness, dignity, and respect. Love everyone, even your enemies. Always return good, even to those who are hostile or hateful.

We often have little or no control over what comes into our lives or how people act toward us, but we always have control over how we respond. Keeping our well's pipeline clear is up to us. When we chose to live righteously, we will experience the benefits and blessings that righteousness brings. Commit yourself consciously and deliberately to think and live righteously. If you do, no evil planned against you will succeed. Your business will flourish while others' are struggling. A way will be made for you where no way seemed possible. You will experience abundant provision when others around you are suffering shortages.

Ten Keys to Releasing Your Potential

At this point, you must be aware of the tremendous wealth of potential locked away inside of you crying out for exposure and fulfillment. I believe you have heard the voices of your childhood dreams and the many visions, goals, and plans you once had screaming out for resurrection. Now the big question remains: *How do I release my potential?*

As mentioned previously, every manufacturer establishes the specifications, environment, conditions, and operational standards for attaining the maximum performance level of his product. After many years of careful study and practice, I have identified ten major keys to releasing your full potential. Violation of any one of these requirements will result in the malfunction, distortion, misuse, and abuse of your precious potential.

The keys to releasing your potential follow:

Key #1.   You must know your Source.

I believe it is essential that you understand the nature, composition, and consistency of your Source, because this is the key to understanding the potency of your potential. If you, for example, had a wooden table in your house, you would be aware that the table is made of wood from a tree. The strength, durability, and nature of the table can only be as strong and durable as the tree. If the tree is weak, the table will be the same. Therefore, the potential of the table is determined by the potential of the source from which it came.

The same is true for you. To understand how much potential you possess, you must understand the Source from which you came. You possess all the qualities and nature of your Source and are capable of manifesting these qualities. You also possess an eternal spirit just like your Source.

Key #2. You must understand how the product was designed to function.

Every manufacturer designs, develops, and produces his or her product to function in a specific manner. Automobile manufacturers design their products to function with gasoline, sparkplugs, batteries, pistons, oil, water, etc. No matter what you do, if you do not supply the elements required for the operational function of the product, it will not perform and maximize its potential.

You were created to function by faith and love. These are the fuels on which we run. The just live (operate) by faith—faith in our Source, ourselves, our potential. Our potential cannot be released without faith and love. Fear and hatred cause the short circuit of our potential.

Key #3. You must know your purpose.

Every product exists for a specific purpose. That reason is the original intent of its existence—the purpose for which the manufacturer made it. This is an essential key because the purpose for which something was made determines its design, nature, and potential.

You were created with a specific purpose in mind. Whatever that purpose is, you possess the potential to fulfill it. No matter how big the dream you have, your potential is equal to the assignment. Purpose gives birth to responsibility, and responsibility makes demands on potential.

Key #4.   You must understand your resources.

All manufacturers provide access to the necessary resources for the proper maintenance, sustenance, and operation of their products. Resources and provisions are to help sustain the product while its potential is being maximized.

You have been provided tremendous material and physical resources to sustain and maintain you as you proceed in realizing, developing, and maximizing your potential. Resources were created to live on and with, but never for. You are never to idolize the resources, nor are you to become controlled by them. Idolatry and substance and drug abuse are violations of the Manufacturer's specifications, and will lead to the destruction of potential.

Key #5.   You must have the right environment.

Environment consists of the conditions that have a direct or indirect effect on the performance, function, and development of a thing. These conditions can be internal and external. Every manufacturer specifies the proper conditions under which he or she guarantees the maximum performance of the potential of the product. In the manual, the manufacturer will caution against violation of that specified environment for maximum performance. The right environment is the ideal conditions needed for the maximization of the true potential.

Everything flourishes within a specific environment. Plants, animals, and fish all need a specific environment in order to live. Potential is nullified, aborted, and destroyed when the environment is violated or disrupted. This is also true of humankind.

You were designed to function best in a positive environment of fellowship, relationship, love, and challenge in order to be maximized. You can never be all you could be in any other environment. The current world environment has poisoned the atmosphere of your potential. It has produced abnormal behavior and the malfunction of the human factor. The key to releasing your true potential is the restoration of the original environment through your internal spiritual environment.

Key #6.   You must work out your potential.

Potential is dormant ability. But ability is useless until it is given responsibility. Work is a major key to releasing your potential. Potential must be exercised and demands made on it, otherwise it will remain potential. Claiming a promise does not make it happen. You must apply the principle of work. Good ideas do not bring success—good, hard work does. To release your true potential, you must be willing to work.

Key #7.   You must cultivate your potential.

Potential is like a seed. It is buried ability and hidden power that need to be cultivated. You must feed your potential the fertilizer of good, positive company and give it the environment of encouragement. Read materials that stimulate your faith, encourage your self-confidence, and nourish your dreams and goals.

Key #8. You must guard your potential.

It is tragic when a tree dies in a seed or a man dies in a boy. It is sad when what could have been becomes what should have been. With all the wealth of your potential, you must be careful to guard and protect it. You must guard your visions and dreams from evil, discouragement, procrastination, failures, opinions, distractions, traditions, and compromise. Others may be after your potential. Be on guard.

Key #9. You must share your potential.

The heavens and earth exist within the potential principle, which can only be fulfilled when it is shared. Nature abounds with this truth. The sun does not exist for itself. Plants release oxygen for you and you give carbon dioxide to the plants. The bee receives nectar as it pollinates the flowers. No potential exists for itself. This is also true of you. True potential and fulfillment in life is not what is accomplished, but who benefits from them. Your deposit was given to enrich and inspire the lives of others. Remember, the great law is love.

Key #10. You must know and understand the laws of limitation.

Freedom and power are two of the most important elements in your life. Potential is the essence of both.

Potential is power. But freedom needs law to be enjoyed, and power needs responsibility to be effective. One without the other produces self-destruction.

Every manufacturer establishes laws of limitations for products. These laws are not given to restrict but to protect, not to hinder but to assist and guarantee the full and maximum performance of potential. There are laws and standards set to protect your potential and to secure your success. Obedience is protection for potential.

All the above keys and principles are proven throughout human history to be true. Any violation of these laws limits the release and maximization of your potential. Take each to heart, and then watch your life unfold dramatically as you discover the hidden ability that was always within you.

Chapter 9

DARE TO BELIEVE
IN YOUR POTENTIAL

Human potential without right
purpose produces self-destruction.

What Are You Doing With Your Potential?

Humankind has accomplished many things. There are many inventors in the world. Many people do great feats and accomplish great exploits. Imagine that you are one of them. Do all you can dream. If you can think it, you can do it.

Yet many of us still live below the level of our true ability. We have settled for the standards established by the opinions of others regarding our potential. We are afraid to move beyond our dreams to action. It is more comfortable to think about all we *might* do instead of working to achieve what we *can* do. People who change the world are people who stop dreaming and wake up. They don't just wish, they act.

I'm here to encourage you to move on with the real things of life. What have you done since your last accomplishment? What new goals have you set?

Life Is More Than Shelter, Food, and Security

Maslow, one of the greatest influences on the thought patterns of psychology in our world, theorized that man is driven by his base needs. He believed that your most immediate need becomes your controlling factor. Therefore, your first instinct is to find shelter; second, food; and third, security or protection. Then you begin to move up the ladder of becoming self-realized and self-actualized, of developing self-esteem, and all the rest of that stuff. According to this theory, human beings are driven by their base needs.

It has been my experience, though, that we should live from the perspective of what exists that we cannot see, instead of being totally caught up in the details and needs of our daily lives. We should live and think in the potential. We should always see things that have not yet been manifested. Faith lives in the potential, not in the present. We need to have faith in the future, in our potential to bring about something better.

Stop worrying. When you realize that food, drink, clothes, and shelter are not the most important things in life, you will realize that there is more—and you can make it happen. When you make the "more" of life happen, all the other basics of life fall into place, into proper perspective.

I believe that Maslow was wrong. There are people who have everything material, but they still don't know who they are. People accumulate things with the hope that the things will make them somebody. But you don't become somebody by accumulating things. Ask the guy at the top who can't sleep. Ask the gal who has everything except peace and love and joy in her heart. Maslow was wrong. You must have a realistic view of your self-worth and self-esteem first. You must know who you are first.

Are You Successful?

Everybody everywhere wants to be "successful," but only very few people succeed. Millions are driven, possessed, and preoccupied with this passion. They would sacrifice anything to be seen or accepted as "successful."

Success in today's world is usually defined by the superficial rewards glorified in the media: wealth, power, fame, luxury, prestige, and recognition. Yet few of us have a firm idea what it takes to be or feel successful. It is easy to presume that a young corporate executive who rises to the top management position of a major corporation and earns nearly a million dollars a year is successful, but would the young man agree? That depends largely on the sacrifices he made to get to the top, the quality of his life outside work, and perhaps most significantly, his personal reason for pursuing his particular career.

If the young man has a positive sense of direction that encompasses his whole life—not just his professional career or bankbook—and if he understands why he wants what he wants, his accomplishments may give him genuine satisfaction, making him a success in his own eyes. If, however, he does not have this sense of fulfillment or clarity of purpose, and especially if he has been struggling to live up to someone else's definition of success—be it that of a parent, a spouse, or perhaps society in general—he is likely to reach the top of his professional ladder, but wonder why he feels so dissatisfied and burned out.

In the end, he may realize that his identity as an individual has been compromised by the forces pushing him to attain career stardom. He has become trapped by the pressure to get ahead, and his life is out of balance. There are millions like this young executive who are striving daily after a prize they despise to accomplish a goal they personally hate.

We, as a society, have confused success with fulfillment, accomplishment with satisfaction, and achievement with peace. I believe it is essential for you and for me to look beyond the wonderful things material success can buy to the heavy price it can exact. You must question why you are so driven to succeed and why you've made the choices and the sacrifices that have shaped your private and professional life thus far.

Can you recall the personal goals that motivated you before external success became your life's ambition? Do you remember the origins of your assumptions about success? After you've traced the development of your personal definition of success, you must consider what it means to be true to yourself—and to take that next step to expose an even better you.

Few of us ever stop to develop a personal and meaningful definition of success that allows us to thrive as well as strive. Instead, we absorb a composite of largely superficial illusions from the media, parental demands, and peer pressure. *In essence, success in our culture requires becoming what everyone else tells you to be.* It is assumed, almost as an afterthought, that success by the world's standards will magically include happiness, but this formula leaves little room for genuine personal fulfillment.

Most people look at those who appear to be successful and think they would be fools to change their jobs or lifestyles, even if they hate what they are doing. Not surprisingly, life dominated day after day, year after year, and one step up the ladder after another by this quest for success becomes increasingly less satisfying and more anxious. Millions of people live at this critical point, trapped between external success and internal collapse. In simple terms, success is not as simple as we once thought.

Success Defined

What is success? By now it must be obvious that I am questioning the world's perception of success. Success has very little to do with what you accumulate, possess, or achieve. It has even less to do with other people's opinions and their assessment of you and your accomplishments. *Success can only be defined by fulfilling your potential and purpose, measured by obedience.* The following statements (worth repeating) support this premise:

- Purpose is the original intent for the creation of a thing. It is the reason and *why* for its existence. Purpose is the "assignment" that is produced by the intent of the creator or manufacturer.

- Completion of the intended assignment is the fulfillment of the reason for existence. Being true to the original intent is the essence of obedience and the measure of faithfulness.

- The satisfaction and pleasure of the manufacturer when the product fulfills his intended purpose is the measure of success.

- Success is the fulfillment and the completion of the original intent for the creation or the production of a product.

- Success is obedience to purpose.

• Success is not what you have done compared to what others have done, but what you have done compared to what you were supposed to do.

These statements show that success has more to do with *being* than *doing*. To be successful is to *finish the originally intended assignment according to the plan and the specifications of the creator*. Fulfilling your potential's purpose is thus the key and the foundation of success. It is the only true source of contentment and the only accurate measurement of life. Therefore, success cannot be determined by the opinions of others about your actions.

You are not successful if everyone says you are. You are not successful if you have done what others expected you to do. You are not successful if you receive commendation and recognition from your peers or the accolades of the masses. You are truly successful only if you have fulfilled your potential and have done what you were purposed to do.

Purpose is doing not a *good* thing, but the *right* thing. As "the best" is the enemy of "the good," so the enemy of "the right thing" is "a good thing." It is dangerous to do a good thing at the expense of the right thing.

Be careful not to confuse *right* with good, famous, big, easy, acceptable, or popular. Your only responsibility is to respond to your purpose for your life. Your only measure of *success* is to fulfill your potential for your life! Living with purpose is the difference between being busy and being effective.

Don't let the tragedy of faithfulness to the wrong thing waste your life. Refuse to allow activity without progress to dominate your existence. Purpose protects you from doing good at the expense of doing right.

You Don't Need Things to Enjoy Life. You Need Life to Enjoy Things.

I have met so many people who have everything except the knowledge of who they are. Life is so much more than the things you worry about. Life is peace, love, joy, patience, and gentleness. When you put these things first in your life, everything else you need will just fall into place.

Peace is so important to a fulfilled life. You don't have to worry when you know what is coming. You don't have to worry if you know how a particular situation is going to turn out. Relax and commit yourself to maximize your potential. Preoccupy yourself with your assignment and purpose for your life, knowing that success has already been provided.

What's Really Important?

When we are distracted by our drive for personal security and our search for identity, we rarely achieve our true potential. Our search for things, what we can relate to through our senses and our minds, harasses us and keeps us so busy trying to make a living that we don't have time to live. We are so caught up trying to make it *through* life that we don't have time to be *in* life.

Have you ever seen people who work all day, every day, and then suddenly they realize they've grown old and can no longer enjoy life? They have missed living because they were so busy trying to make one.

Your potential is not determined by how much money is in your bank account or what title is on your business card. Nor is it determined by what others think and expect from you. You have the power to determine the extent of your ability and to develop and experience your entire potential. Although you may not look smart or creative or agile, but if that's what it takes to fulfill your potential—those traits are already within you somewhere.

Potential Produces Faith. Faith Is Knowing Potential Is There.

Faith is being sure of what we hope for and certain of what we don't see. Faith deals with potential—what you yet can see, do, be, and experience. Faith says, "I can't see it, but I believe it is there." Faith never deals with what you have done, but with what you yet could do.

But you have to live with faith, because faith is the stuff that deals with unseen things. Faith is not some spooky experience. It's simply knowing that what you can't see is there.

Can you imagine waking up every day, with all your problems, knowing that whatever you see is not the real story? Can you even imagine living that way—looking not at things that can be seen, but at the things that are not seen? What we see is temporary. It's those things we can't see that are eternal. Living by faith requires looking at the unseen; everything you could be is in you now, waiting for you to make demands on it by faith.

Wishing Is Not Enough—Dare to Desire

Have you misread the word *desire*? We have expected, perhaps, that the word *desire* means what we are dreaming about. No. Desire is craving enough to sacrifice for. Only if we are willing to die for what we desire will we receive it.

Desire is craving enough to sacrifice for.

How often have you had a good idea and done nothing about it because you didn't desire it badly enough? When we want something so strongly we can taste it, an urgency energizes our efforts. This is extremely important for your faith, because faith is what you are asking for but can't yet see. A strong desire enables you to stand your ground until you see what you have believed.

There are only a few who are gutsy enough to live in this manner. How much do you really desire the goals you have set for your life?

When you ask for something in faith, it is already on the way. You can't see it, but if you believe, it is already in process. But you must not just desire it, you must, as discussed previously, work to make it happen.

Your Desire Controls Your Direction in Life

Many people get distracted in life because they do not desire anything enough to keep on course. If you do not set a goal for your potential and say, "Look, I don't care what anybody says. That's what I want to become," you might as well forget it. You must have a goal that you desire so strongly that you will go after it no matter what the expense. If you are not willing to do that, you have lost already, because it is your desire for the thing that will keep you on the road of consistency. Potential needs desire to place demands upon it.

**You must have a goal you desire
so strongly you will go after it
no matter what the expense.**

This life is full of advertisements for your attention. Life is crowded and jammed with distractions. They come from all sides, trying to shake you from your goal. If you don't have a goal, they will provide one for you. You must know where you want to go and what you want to become. Potential needs purpose to give it direction.

Refuse to be distracted or interrupted. The power of your potential will be revealed as you sacrifice everything to attain what you desire.

Potential Fulfilled for Only a Few

Unfortunately, many will never fulfill their deepest desires. They will fall prey to false attitudes and perceptions that keep them from achieving their real potential. How disappointing.

Perhaps you are a parent who has tried and tried and tried and still your kids don't have productive lives. You've tried your best and given your best, but they still have disappointed you. Many employers feel this way. They give and give and give opportunities, and the people still disappoint them. And often some of the ones who are messing up the most are the ones to whom they have given the most. Each of us feels the hurt when the people we love and have tried to help, struggle in the gutter—their lives in ruins.

I want all who read this book to fulfill their potential; but I know only a few will. Only a minute percentage of those who hear the message about who they are will ever become all they could be. Many people will never fulfill their purpose in life. They will not be who they were supposed to be or achieve what they were designed to do. It's terrible to say, but that's why I'm sharing this with you. If only I could take my desire and put it into you, I'd do it. But I can't. Some readers may end up in the gutter because they won't receive and practice what they've read. I'm sorry, but it will happen.

Whether you fail or succeed, win or lose, does not depend on anyone but you. You must be willing to unclog the well, have faith, and work to fulfill your potential in life.

Be One of the Few

Not everyone will look for the things planted within them to reach their destiny. Not everyone will choose to fulfill their potential. Indeed, the number will be few.

I wonder where you are. Are you going through the broad gate where everybody is going nowhere? Are you one of the many who aren't going to be anything more than they are today?

Come, join the ones journeying through the narrow gate. Be one of the few. Decide you're not going with the crowd. Separate yourself, square your shoulders, and do something. Choose to be somebody instead of nobody. Leave your footprints in the sands of history and carry none of your potential to the cemetery.

It is true that few will dare to take the challenge to live an abundant life. That's terrible. I wish that none should perish, but it is only a wish.

Are you going to join the other guys? Are you going to be any different from the other young girls? Are you going to give in to your base nature and mess up your life getting lost so no one can ever find you? Are you going to be one of those people whose grave has to be marked to make sure everyone knows you used to live on this planet?

Or are we going to be compelled to remember you because you made your mark on history? Will you decide that you are going to build so many monuments in people's lives that they won't have to put a stone on your grave to remind us you lived?

Don't join the crowd—you'll get lost. Be different. Stick out like a sore thumb. Join the few.

The United States Marines established a recruiting standard that expresses this attitude: "We want a few good men." They don't want everybody or anybody. They want "the few, the proud, the Marines."

Crowds don't excite me. It's those few who I see still working on it 20 years later who excite me. They are still there plugging away. It's the few who don't allow disappointment to disarm them. They are motivated by their failure and refuse to quit until they're finished.

Are you a can-do person? Are you brave enough to face the challenge and take the risk to be effective? Will you dare to believe the impossible no matter what others say? I hope so. The world desperately needs people who will go for the miracles no matter what it takes. The world needs people who will believe for the potential buried within them—desiring their dreams enough to move out and act.

Only a few will find the kind of potential that allows them to live from the depths of their hidden ability. But for those who do, deep wells of possibilities will come to light.

Join the few. Release the miracles hidden in your thoughts. Dare to try again and again even after you've failed. Become reconnected to God and find out who you are and what you can do. Give your potential a chance—you can do much more than you can think or imagine. Become the beautiful, successful, joyful person you were created to be.

A Parting Word

The World Within the Third World

Today there are almost seven billion people on planet Earth. Over half of these people live in countries and conditions that have been labeled Third World. This term was invented by a French economist who was attempting to describe the various groupings of peoples throughout the world based on their socio-economic status. Whether or not this term is valid, it is generally accepted as a description or element of identification for millions of people.

I was born and live in a part of the world that is said to fall within this category. The term is defined as any people who did not benefit from or participate in the industrial revolution. A large majority of these people were not allowed to benefit from or participate in the industrial revolution because they were subjugated at that time, being used to fuel the economic base for that revolution. Many of them were reduced to slaves and indentured servants, thus robbing them of their identity, dignity, self-worth, and self-respect.

A Word to the Victims of History

Today, despite changes in conditions and a greater measure of freedom and independence, many people are still grappling with their identity and their sense of self-worth. Many of the nations that progressed and developed through the industrial revolution have reinforced (by attitudes, policies, and legislations) the notion that Third World people do not possess the potential to develop the skills, intelligence, and sophistication necessary to equal that of industrialized states.

With this prejudice in mind, I wish to say to all Third World peoples everywhere—black, yellow, brown, red, and white; African, American, Indian, Spanish, Latin, Arabian, Asian, and other nationalities—your potential is limitless. You possess the ability to achieve, develop, accomplish, produce, create, and perform anything your mind can conceive. You were created with all the potential you need deposited within you so you can fulfill your potential in this life.

The opinions of others should never determine your self-worth. Your identity is not found in the prejudgments of others. The wealth within the Third World must be realized, harnessed, and maximized by its people. We must be willing to work and commit ourselves to tapping the potential within the land, our youth, the arts, sports, and music. Our governments must believe that they have the ability to improve on systems and forms institutionalized by the industrialized states. The Third World must begin to take responsibility for its own people and appreciate that they have the potential to write their own songs and books and to develop an indigenous curriculum for education, leadership training, resource management, and financial autonomy and accountability.

It is crucial that we do not inhibit our potential to chart a new course for the future by being destroyed by our preoccupation with the past. We have the responsibility to deposit the wealth of our potential in this generation so the next generation can build their future on our faithfulness to becoming everything we can possibly be. Just as there is a forest in every seed, so I am certain there is a new world within your world.

EXCITING TITLES

by
Dr. Myles Munroe

UNDERSTANDING YOUR POTENTIAL

This is a motivating, provocative look at the awesome potential trapped within you, waiting to be realized. This book will cause you to be uncomfortable with your present state of accomplishment and dissatisfied with resting on your past success.

RELEASING YOUR POTENTIAL

Here is a complete, integrated, principles-centered approach to releasing the awesome potential trapped within you. If you are frustrated by your dreams, ideas, and visions, this book will show you a step-by-step pathway to releasing your potential and igniting the wheels of purpose and productivity.

MAXIMIZING YOUR POTENTIAL

Are you bored with your latest success? Maybe you're frustrated at the prospect of retirement. This book will refire your passion for living! Learn to maximize the God-given potential lying dormant inside you through the practical, integrated, and penetrating concepts shared in this book. Go for the max—die empty!

SINGLE, MARRIED, SEPARATED & LIFE AFTER DIVORCE

Written by best-selling author Myles Munroe, this is one of the most important books you will ever read. It answers hard questions with compassion, biblical truth, and even a touch of humor. It, too, has been a best seller.

IN PURSUIT OF PURPOSE

Best-selling author Myles Munroe reveals here the key to personal fulfillment: purpose. We must pursue purpose because our fulfillment in life depends upon our becoming what we were born to be and do. *In Pursuit of Purpose* will guide you on that path to finding purpose.

THE PURPOSE AND POWER OF PRAISE & WORSHIP

God's greatest desire and humankind's greatest need is for a Spirit-to-spirit relationship. God created an environment of His Presence in which man is to dwell and experience the fullness of this relationship. In this book, Dr. Munroe will help you discover this experience in your daily life. You are about to discover the awesome purpose and power of praise and worship.

THE PURPOSE AND POWER OF GOD'S GLORY

Everywhere we turn, we are surrounded by glory. There is glory in every tree and flower. There is the splendor in the rising and setting sun. Every living creature reflects its own glory. Man in his own way through his actions and character expresses an essence of glory. But the glory that we see in creation is but the barest reflection of the greater glory of the Creator. Dr. Munroe surgically removes the religious rhetoric out of this most-oft used word, replacing it with words that will draw you into the powerful presence of the Lord. *The Purpose and Power of God's Glory* not only introduces you to the power of the glory but practically demonstrates how God longs to see His glory reflected through humankind.

Available at your local bookstore, from www.destinyimage.com or www.amazon.com.

For more information and sample chapters, visit www.destinyimage .com.